COMPUT
AND THEIR USE

An introduction

Lionel Carter is a qualified Chartered Mechanical Engineer and Principal Lecturer in Management Science at Slough College of Higher Education.

Dr Eva Huzan is Head of the Computing Division at Slough College of Higher Education, a member of the Computing Science Advisory Panel ('O' and 'A' level), University of London, and a Fellow of the British Computer Society.

The authors have collaborated before in writing *Learn Computer Programming with the Commodore VIC-20*, and Teach Yourself books on *The Pocket Calculator, Microelectronics and Microcomputers, Computer Programming in BASIC* and *Computer Programming with the Commodore 64*.

TEACH YOURSELF BOOKS

COMPUTERS AND THEIR USE

An introduction

L. R. Carter and E. Huzan

TEACH YOURSELF BOOKS
Hodder and Stoughton

First published 1984
Third impression 1988

British Library Cataloguing in Publication Data
Carter, L. R.
Computers and their use.
1. Electronic digital computers
   I. Title   II. Huzan, E.
   001.64   QA76.5

ISBN 0 340 35652 9

Printed and bound in Great Britain
for Hodder and Stoughton Educational,
a division of Hodder and Stoughton Ltd,
Mill Road, Dunton Green, Sevenoaks, Kent,
by Richard Clay Ltd, Bungay, Suffolk.
Photoset by Rowland Phototypesetting Ltd,
Bury St Edmunds, Suffolk

Contents

List of Figures

Introduction

This book is intended as a general introduction to the wide variety of computer equipment and applications currently available.

Many computers, usually microcomputers, are now used in offices, schools and in the home. As well as using microcomputers for learning programming in different languages, the full potential of these machines can be realised through the use of ready-made programs called *software packages*.

A very common use of computers in offices is for word processing. This provides an efficient means of preparing reports and standard letters which can easily be altered by making the changes on the computer's screen, and then storing the revised document on a disk file. Documents can be printed when required, as 'perfect' copies.

In addition, microcomputers may be used in offices for business planning and data processing. By linking the computers together in a network, users can send messages to each other both within the company and externally, using electronic mail facilities. School and home users also can *access* (obtain) external information held on computer systems through the telephone, using adapted television sets or their microcomputers with a special attachment. The information accessed may be concerned, for example, with finance, the weather or entertainment, or may be *telesoftware* – programs that can be 'downloaded' into the microcomputer's memory.

Inexpensive word processing and business-type packages are also available for the school and home user. However, one of the most popular uses of home computers is for games, which use the computer's colour graphics and sound facilities. If you have a home computer, you can learn to program your machine, through books or college courses, and develop your own applications for entertainment or keeping records, such as details of club membership.

Another area that is being developed in schools is concerned with control applications, that is, using microcomputers to control equipment, or to program a robot arm for picking up and placing down objects.

Robots are used in industry for automating processes which are repetitive, or those which need to be carried out in conditions not fit for people to work in. The design of equipment can be aided by the use of computers, as can many of the manufacturing processes, and the planning and control of projects.

Some of the uses of computers are linked to social issues; benefits can be gained by using computers in health care and to help the disabled. However, because so much information is being stored in computers, great care must be taken to make sure that people not entitled to see the information cannot gain access to it. This involves using special techniques to prevent unauthorised access, and also legislation to control the setting up of data files and use of information contained in them.

Today you are likely to come into contact with computers in your everyday life, for example when paying bills or using cash cards. These systems will have been designed and programmed by computer professionals. However, computing is no longer just the province of the specialist. You may have access to a computer yourself which you can use as a source of entertainment, for extending your knowledge, or for improving your business. This book has been written to help you to understand how computers can be used to achieve these aims. There is an overview at the beginning of each chapter which you can read first to give you a preliminary understanding of the subject before you go on to the more detailed material.

It is usual to cite the owners of the trademarks of software products when describing them, and these are listed below:

CP/M is a trademark of Digital Research;

MSDOS is a trademark of Microsoft;

PCDOS is a trademark of IBM;

UCSD Pascal is a trademark of the Regents of the University of California at San Diego;

UNIX is a trademark of Bell Laboratories;

WordStar is a trademark of MicroPro International.

1

Computer Equipment

Overview

Most of today's computers work on principles invented many years ago. The earliest business computers were developed around 1950. Since then the main developments have been concerned with improvements in the power and reliability of the equipment.

The need for very small electronic circuits of great reliability was established by organisations concerned with sending equipment into space, where the weight of the missile was a prime consideration. However, once the technology for fabricating microelectronic circuits was perfected, its potential use in the industrial and business sectors provided a huge new market for further exploitation.

Microelectronic devices are made from wafer-thin pieces of a material such as silicon. A small chip of silicon, a few millimetres square, can contain a very large number of electronic components built into circuits. These chips are called *integrated circuits*. Microchips, such as the one shown in Figure 1.1, are used in all types of computer equipment in both large and small systems.

The effect of the 'micro revolution' is seen in the office, on the shop floor, in schools, and in the home, where inexpensive microcomputers can be used for a wide range of applications. The larger computers have been reduced in size, and have also become more powerful by the use of microelectronic components in their construction. The increased capabilities, across the whole range of computers, include large magnetic storage capacities, good quality printers, colour graphic displays, and easier interaction with the computer by devices such as light pens. There is also widespread use of character recognition and bar code equipment for entering information rapidly into computers.

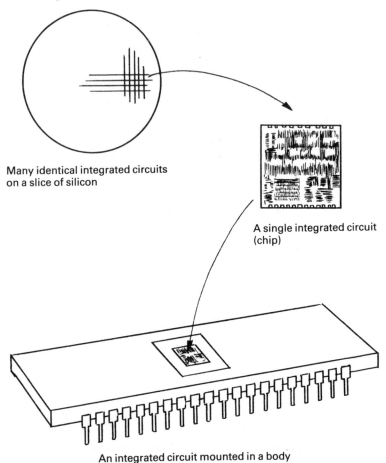

Many identical integrated circuits
on a slice of silicon

A single integrated circuit
(chip)

An integrated circuit mounted in a body
(DIP – Dual Inline Package)

Figure 1.1   Stages in the production of an integrated circuit

Basic units and functions

Figure 1.2 shows the basic units of a computer. The main store or
memory is used to hold programs and data. A *program* is a set of
instructions to perform a particular task. For example, Figure 1.3
shows a very simple program to add some numbers. This has been
written in a programming language called BASIC (Beginners All-
purpose Symbolic Instruction Code).

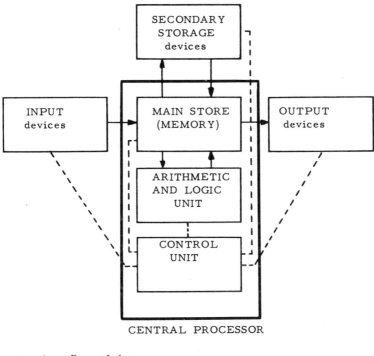

flow of data
control links

Figure 1.2 Basic units of a computer

The program is entered into the memory of the computer by pressing the appropriate keys on the keyboard (the *input* device). Once the program is in the computer's memory, keying in a command, such as RUN, will cause the computer to start executing (obeying) the program instructions. The program instructions, and any other commands and computer responses, are displayed on the computer's screen (monitor) or *visual display unit* (VDU), which is the *output* device.

The INPUT instruction asks for three numbers to be entered (in response to the question mark). The computer works out the answer very quickly using its *arithmetic and logic unit*, so that the sum of the numbers is displayed immediately. The program can be run as many times as required, with other numbers, including those

```
10 INPUT "ENTER THREE NUMBERS";A,B,C
20 S=A+B+C
30 PRINT
40 PRINT "THE SUM IS";S
50 END

RUN
ENTER THREE NUMBERS ?4,7,9

THE SUM IS 20
READY
```

Figure 1.3   A simple program to add three numbers

with decimal places. The program and results could be printed out using a printer as an alternative output device.

Programs used in business will be very much longer – for example, many thousands of instructions for a large payroll program. These programs are keyed in just once, and recorded onto magnetic disks. The programs can then be tested and corrected by loading them from the disk into the computer's memory. The data to be used with the programs may also be stored on disk.

Smaller programs used on microcomputers can be saved on low-cost disks or cassette tape. Magnetic tape or disk units are known as *backing* or *secondary storage* devices, because they back-up the computer's main memory.

The various parts of the computer send and receive signals at electronic speeds, and it is vital that the speeds and synchronisation of the signals are accurately controlled. This is the function of the *control unit*.

The central part of the computer – memory, arithmetic and logic unit (ALU), and control unit – is known as its *central processor* or *central processing unit* (CPU).

How information is held

Information is stored in computers in binary form. Binary digits have either the value one or zero and can be represented within the computer by just two states, examples of which are high and low levels of voltage or north–south and south–north magnetic fields. Any two-state system can be used to represent the zero and one binary values.

Zero and one binary digits are called *bits* (from binary digits). The term *byte* is used to mean a group of eight bits, and much computer circuitry is designed to process information in bytes. With some computers the unit of data handled by the circuitry is a *word*, which is usually made up of several bytes. For example, a 32-bit word is made up of four bytes.

All letters of the alphabet, other characters such as punctuation, and numbers have to be coded into binary before the computer can make use of them. A commonly used code is the ASCII code (American Standard Code for Information Interchange). In this code, the letter A, for example, is 1000001. An extra bit is added for checking purposes, making eight bits in all.

There are several other coding systems in use, but the ASCII code is the one most frequently used with microcomputers. The encoding is carried out automatically by the equipment, so when a key is pressed on a keyboard, the equivalent ASCII code for that character will be stored automatically in the computer's memory.

All the tangible items of the computer system, that is, those that can be seen and touched, are called *hardware*. The programs, whether stored on tape or disk or in the main memory, are called *software* (as opposed to hardware). Computer software is discussed in Chapter 2, and programming in Chapter 3.

The central processor

The central processor processes the program currently stored in the computer's main memory. A part of the central processor fetches the instructions, one at a time in sequence, from main memory and executes them. The central processor keeps track of progress by storing various types of information in a set of memory cells known as *registers*.

All memory cells are uniquely identified to allow information to be retrieved from where it has been stored. One register called the program counter keeps track of the next instruction to be executed. As the instruction is executed, the required data is fetched from the main memory and stored temporarily in registers called *accumulators*. The result of the calculation is built up in an accumulator prior to transferring it to the main memory. Other registers are used in conjunction with the accumulators to indicate such things as the fact that the result was negative.

In addition to the circuits that perform arithmetic, the central processor also contains control circuits to ensure that the actions taken are synchronised correctly. These circuits are based upon the oscillation of a quartz crystal, as used in quartz clocks and watches.

Computer memory

The memory of the computer consists of two types of microchips – Read Only Memory (ROM) and Random Access Memory (RAM). ROM is a permanent form of memory that contains program instructions in its circuits. The program may be built into the chip when it is manufactured or put later into a chip called a Programmable ROM (PROM) or Erasable PROM (EPROM). The programs held in ROMs or PROMs are permanent and cannot be changed. An EPROM is useful at the development stage of a PROM or ROM. A program can be tried out in the EPROM, and if necessary erased, using ultraviolet light, and corrected until it has been perfected. This is the method often used in research and development laboratories to design ROMs.

A very common use for ROM chips is for storing the software that controls a microcomputer. Some microcomputers allow you to use a programming language (such as BASIC) as soon as you switch on, because the necessary software is contained in a ROM chip. This avoids having to load this software into the computer's RAM from magnetic tape or disk.

Some home computers allow a cartridge to be plugged into an

external socket. These cartridges contain ROM or RAM chips. In the case of ROM-based cartridges, it is a simple way of allowing the user to access additional software contained in the ROMs. Adding RAM cartridges allows the user to extend the basic memory capacity of the computer.

All forms of ROM retain their contents when the computer is switched off. RAM, on the other hand, loses the information stored in it when the computer is switched off. It is therefore used as a short-term memory. RAM is the area of main memory used for holding programs typed in from the keyboard or read in from magnetic tape or disk. When a program is being run, data may need to be input from the keyboard or from magnetic tape or disk; and this data will also be read into RAM.

Microcomputers

Figure 1.4 shows a typical microcomputer system. The central processor of a microcomputer is called a *microprocessor*. Backing storage may consist of a cassette recorder or a disk unit.

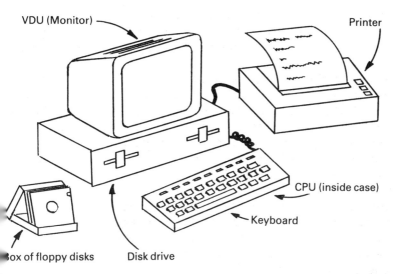

Figure 1.4   A typical microcomputer system

Disk storage

Flexible or floppy disks, and hard disks may be used. Floppy disks are contained in a cardboard sleeve for protection, as shown in Figure 1.5. The disk rotates within its sleeve when the disk is mounted in the disk drive. Information is read from the disk or recorded on (written to) the disk by read/write heads through a slot in the protective sleeve. Different sizes of disk are available: 3 in (7.5 cm), 5¼ in (13 cm), and 8 in (20 cm). The size of the disk does not necessarily indicate the amount of information that can be held on it, since data can be packed more densely to give a higher capacity.

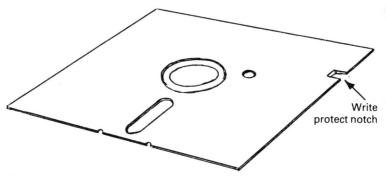

Write protect notch

Figure 1.5   A floppy disk

Recording can be on one or both sides of the floppy disk, depending on the disk drive being used. The disk can be protected from being overwritten by uncovering the *write protect notch* (for 8 in (20 cm) disks) or covering the notch with foil (for 5¼ in (13 cm) disks). The procedure is reversed when information needs to be recorded on the disk.

Floppy disks have the disadvantage of limited storage (100 KB to 1 MB is common). Note that KB stands for *kilobyte*, that is 1024 bytes, and MB stands for *megabytes*, that is 1024 kilobytes. Hard disk units of a similar size to floppy disk units are available with capacities ranging from 5 MB to about 100 MB.

This type of hard disk is based on 'Winchester technology', which means the hard disks are totally enclosed in an airtight box to prevent dust from getting in. Single- or multi-platter Winchesters are available to give the same effect as having a number of separate floppy disks. Information held on Winchester disks may be copied on to floppy disks for security purposes. This may be tedious for large capacity Winchesters. An alternative is to use cartridge tape for back up which can hold the entire contents of, say a 10 MB Winchester.

Printers and plotters

Several different types of printer and plotter may be used with microcomputers; principally, dot matrix, daisy-wheel and ink-jet printers, and graph plotters.

Dot matrix printers

These printers have a printing head made up from a group, or matrix, of needles. This allows any shape character to be printed by activating the appropriate needles to produce the required pattern of dots.

Thermal printers may also use a matrix printing head but require special heat-sensitive paper. Their main advantage is that they are silent in operation as the characters are formed by heating the paper locally to create the image.

Dot matrix printers often contain elaborate options to compete with better quality printers, such as daisy-wheel printers. For example, the print position of adjacent needles in the matrix in some models overlap. Although this means that adjacent needles cannot be activated simultaneously, by activating the printing head twice in the same position, a row of overlapping dots can be produced. This gives the appearance of a continuous line, rather than one made up from dots, making it suitable for printing letters and good-quality reports.

Symbols can be designed with needles on the lines or between the lines for each row. Figure 1.6 shows the needle pattern for an ampersand symbol (&). Less sophisticated printers can only print dots in the spaces.

Note that there are two empty rows at the bottom of the matrix. When the printer is in the 'underline' mode, the bottom row is filled with dots. This again gives a better look to the printed output. Using a less sophisticated printer, the underlining would have to take up the next line on the paper, as it would be a symbol requiring separate printing.

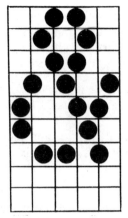

Figure 1.6   A dot matrix character

Other features of matrix printers can include: variable spacing for line feed; a variety of print styles, for example, elite, pica, italic; the ability to define your own character set; and reverse feeding of the paper. Most modern dot matrix printers have many of these features, and contain their own microprocessor and memory, making them programmable. Printing speeds vary considerably, but 100 to 200 characters per second is reasonable for printing fairly long program listings and reports.

Daisy-wheel printers

A commonly used printer for word-processing applications has a circular wheel which moves across the paper. The character set is embossed on the ends of the spokes or 'petals' of the 'daisy-wheel'.

The daisy-wheel printer, being an impact printer, has the advantage of giving electric-typewriter quality printing. Wheels can be interchanged, allowing a wide variety of type-faces and character sets to be used. However, daisy-wheel printers have typical speeds of 30 to 60 characters per second, making them much slower than most matrix printers, and they also tend to be noisy. The noise can be reduced by placing the printer in a soundproof box so that it can be used in offices.

Some daisy-wheel printers have two wheels which can speed up printing or allow two different character sets to be used during a print run. For example, one wheel could have upper and lower case letters and numbers, with mathematical symbols held on a second wheel for technical reports.

Ink-jet printers
These printers can give a good image suitable for word processing. The characters are formed on the paper by a high-speed jet of drops of ink which are electrically charged.

Graph plotters
Continuous line drawings and diagrams can be output to a *graph plotter* (see Figure 1.7). The graph or diagram is produced by coloured pens which can be raised or lowered under computer control. In flat-bed plotters, the paper is stationary and the pens move over the paper, whereas in drum plotters, the paper is driven backwards and forwards while the pens move along a stationary track lying horizontally across the paper. Plotters are available with software for various popular microcomputers. These allow plotter commands to be embedded in programs written, for example, in BASIC.

Printers and other peripheral devices, i.e. equipment which can be attached to the processor, are connected to input/output ports via standard interfaces. Two common standard interfaces are the

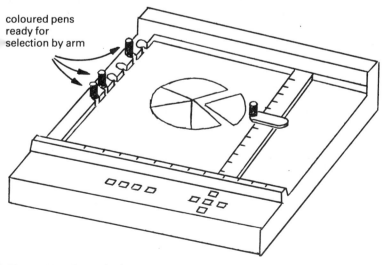

coloured pens
ready for
selection by arm

Figure 1.7 A graph plotter

RS232C serial interface (data is sent as a stream of bits), or the Centronics parallel interface (data is sent in bytes). A third standard interface, the IEEE–488, is used extensively for linking scientific instruments as well as some printers.

Visual display units

The main form of output with a microcomputer is the visual display unit. This unit has a cathode ray tube similar to that in a television set. In fact, with many personal or home computers, you can use your ordinary television as the VDU. The information presented on the screen consists of approximately twenty-five lines of characters. The number of characters on a line varies from about twenty on some microcomputer systems up to about a hundred and thirty on VDUs linked to large computers.

The video output from a microcomputer is commonly fed into the aerial socket of a TV set, as this is the most convenient method of connecting to the TV set. However, this method can lead to a loss of quality in the display, because of the additional processing required on the video signal.

The original video signal in the microcomputer consists of three separate signals. The three signals are for controlling the red, green and blue electron beams that go to make up a coloured TV picture, and this type of signal is referred to as *RGB input/output.*

In transferring these signals from a microcomputer to a TV set, the three signals are often mixed together into a single signal known as *composite video.* If the input to the TV set is to be via the aerial socket, the composite video signal has to be transformed further (by a method called modulation) into an ultra high frequency signal (UHF) similar to broadcast signals received down the aerial to a TV set.

The TV set then repeats the processing, but in the opposite sequence. The signal from the aerial is converted back to a composite video signal (this process is known as demodulation) and the composite signal is then split into its red, green and blue components.

The best quality screen displays are therefore obtained from a microcomputer that has RGB output, used in conjunction with a video unit that accepts RGB direct. The next best quality comes from feeding a composite signal from a microcomputer directly into the appropriate stage of a TV set, bypassing the aerial tuning and demodulating circuits. With the advent of home computers, a number of TV set manufacturers now offer these more direct forms of input.

Low, medium and high resolution monitors are available for use with microcomputers for good quality graphic displays. Each dot, or *pixel*, on the screen can be 'addressed', through program instructions, and joined together so that different figures can be drawn or special characters formed from groups of pixels.

Other specialised video monitors include ones that have touch screens. These units can determine the position of a finger placed against the screen. One method used is to cause the finger to break a matrix of invisible beams projected across the face of the screen. The coordinates of the position of the finger can be determined from breaking particular horizontal and vertical beams.

Distinguishing features of microcomputers

The distinguishing features between one microcomputer and another include the type of microprocessor used, the amount of main memory, graphics, colour and sound capabilities.

Microprocessors are generally classified as 8-bit, 16-bit or 32-bit, which refers to their addressing and data transfer capability. The higher bit processors are capable of directly addressing a much larger main memory (RAM and ROM) and hence can hold much larger programs. They are also more powerful in that they can process computer instructions more quickly.

Large computer systems

Figure 1.8 shows a typical configuration for a large computer system. This could have a large main memory of, say, four megabytes, with several disk units, each holding three to six hundred megabytes of information. This type of storage would typically be required for a time-sharing system, in which many users have access to the central processor, disks and printers via VDU terminals (each with a screen and keyboard). Graphics terminals may also be used; these have high resolution screens for displaying continuous line drawings.

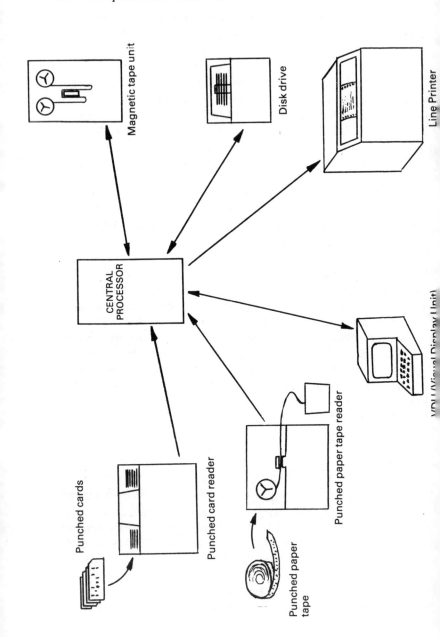

The disks are removable so that programs and data can be stored off-line (*on-line* means there is a direct link to the computer; *off-line* means not currently linked to the computer). Each disk pack has several disks, for example six, mounted on a common central shaft, and separated by a space from each other. The outer surfaces of the disk pack are not used, giving ten recording surfaces for a six-disk pack. Read/write heads move in from the sides towards the centre and back, while the disk pack revolves at a constant speed. Each recording surface of the disk pack is coated with a magnetically sensitive material, and information is recorded magnetically on concentric tracks.

The magnetic tape unit is of the reel-to-reel type. Characters, represented by their bit codes, are recorded magnetically across the width of the tape on a series of tracks. Information is recorded sequentially, that is, from beginning to end along the tape, and has to be accessed sequentially when it is read back into the computer.

Disks enable information to be accessed directly and are essential for most business use. Magnetic tape is used for holding information copied from the disks for archival storage.

The printer shown in Figure 1.8 has a cylindrical printing barrel which is the full width of the paper (up to 132 characters per line). There is a full width inked ribbon between the barrel and the paper. The barrel has a full set of characters (A to Z, etc.) around its circumference in every printing position along its length. The barrel revolves at high speed and at any instant a line of the same characters is opposite the printing hammers which lie behind the paper. This means that if the letter is A, for example, an A can be printed anywhere along the line. A line of printing, therefore, is built up out of sequence, that is, not in a continuous movement from left to right, but is complete after one revolution of the barrel. The printer appears to print a line at a time, and for this reason, it is called a *line printer*.

Punched cards and punched paper tape were the traditional input media used with computers, but now the main method is via the keyboards of VDUs.

Alternative peripherals

For certain applications it is possible to 'automate' the input. Perhaps one of the earliest commercial applications of automating the input of information was the use of Magnetic Ink Character Recognition (MICR) codes printed along the bottom of cheques. In this application, the cheque number, account number and bank branch number are preprinted in a specially designed style of lettering. The ink used can be magnetised, so that when the cheque is passed through an MICR reader, all this preprinted information can be read automatically by the reader, thereby avoiding the need to key it into the computer system.

Cheques can be overstamped by the bank cashier without affecting the validity of the MICR coding, since only magnetised characters are read by the reader. However, the equipment is expensive and the style of lettering is difficult for people to read easily.

An alternative approach has been developed in which typed or printed characters can be read optically using Optical Character Recognition (OCR) readers. The OCR characters are input to a computer by scanning them with light-sensitive heads that 'read' each character. Providing there is sufficient contrast between the printed characters and the background, the heads can sense and decode the printing. This approach enables the computer to produce printed output using OCR characters. For example, bills can be printed by the computer, circulated, read by the recipient, and then further entries can be made on the form after payment. Finally, the completed form can be resubmitted to the computer system to be read automatically without the need for keyboard entry.

Bar codes and magnetic stripe

Other ways of automatically reading information into the computer include bar codes and magnetic stripes. A lot of grocery items now have bar codes printed on their packaging. These codes appear as a collection of thin and thick black lines separated by spaces. When a light-sensitive pen is passed along the bar code, the pattern of light reflected by the bar code to a sensor in the head of the pen can be decoded by the bar code reader unit.

Magnetic stripe is a similar idea, but the code is recorded on a short narrow stripe of magnetic material that looks similar to magnetic tape, and is usually incorporated as part of a price label. When the item is sold, a *wand* (hand-held pen) is passed over the ticket and all the recorded details are read into a point of sale (POS) terminal, which looks like a cash register, and is linked to a computer (see Chapter 7).

These two methods are useful in shops and similar situations because they are quicker and more accurate than having to enter the data by hand at a keyboard.

Light pens

A light pen can also be used in conjunction with a visual display unit. The VDU screen or TV screen is constantly being scanned at high speed by a beam of light. If a light sensitive pen is held against the screen, it registers a signal as the beam passes by. From a knowledge of the speed of the beam and the signal from the pen, the computer can calculate the position of the pen on the screen's surface. This leads to the following uses.

In many computer applications, the user needs to select from a list of options, for example, add a personnel record, delete a personnel record, update a personnel record. By displaying the choice on the screen and requesting the user to point to the required alternative with a light pen, the computer can determine which alternative was selected (see Figure 1.9). A touch screen could also be used for this type of application.

Another use of light pens is associated with Computer Aided Design (CAD). If a light pen is moved across the surface of a VDU screen, the computer can determine its path and display a trace accordingly. As described above, the sketches on the screen would look inaccurate and freehand. CAD applications take the idea further by allowing the user to select the type of line required, for example, straight, or arc of a circle, either by keyboard entry, or as previously described from a selection on the screen. If, for example, a straight line was selected, the light pen would then be positioned in turn at the two ends of the required line. The computer would then draw a straight line between these points.

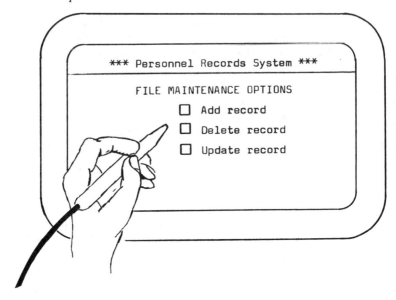

Figure 1.9   Using a light pen

Digitising pad

A further method of inputting information into a computer is by means of a digitising pad. Under the surface, the pad consists of a large matrix of pressure sensitive elements, similar in some respects to the dots on a TV screen. When writing on the surface, the computer is receiving from the pad the equivalent of a dot to dot diagram of the path of the pen. Providing the writing is neat and in the prescribed style, the computer can determine the intended letters. An advantage of this type of device is that it is alphabet independent, as the computer can be programmed to 'understand' special symbols written on the pad.

Digital tracer

Details of a plan, map, etc., can be input to a computer by tracing over the original using a digital tracer, as shown in Figure 1.10. The microcomputer determines the coordinates of the crosswire in the movable head of the tracer by interpreting the signals from 'angular transducers' built into the two movable joints.

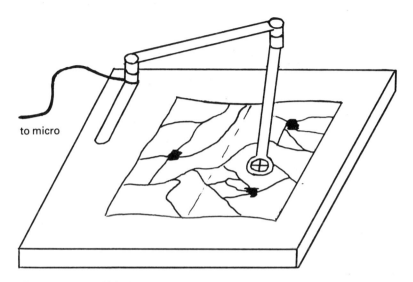

to micro

Figure 1.10 A digital tracer

Joystick

A joystick, such as the one shown in Figure 1.11, may be used for games which require the player to steer an object around the screen. Joysticks used with microcomputers are similar to those used with television games and usually allow movement along two axes (up/down, left/right), and there may also be a pushbutton as a 'fire' control. The simplest joysticks simply 'switch on' the movement, say upwards, when the joystick is moved in the up direction, and give no control over the speed of movement. The more elaborate joysticks have proportional controls, that is, the further the joystick is moved in any direction, the faster the object on the screen moves in that direction.

Image processing

Input of images to a computer is achieved by using video cameras techniques whereby the image received through the lens is digitally processed. A video camera pointed at a photograph, a group of objects or a general scene translates the optical rays into digital signals. These signals can be used to display a digitised 'picture' on

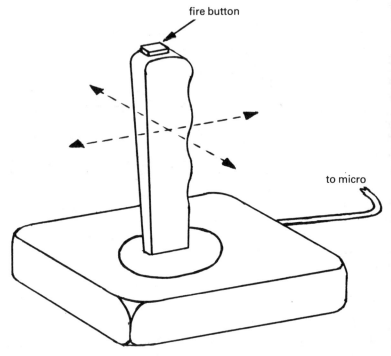

Figure 1.11   A joystick

the screen of a VDU or monitor, or alternatively they can be stored in the normal way on magnetic disk for later viewing or further processing. Computerised 'enhancement' of such digitised pictures can often make certain details clearer by emphasis of tonal boundaries in the picture and the elimination of background 'noise'. These techniques are used routinely in satellite photography and space exploration.

Communications

Early computers required that all data that needed to be input to the computer was delivered to a data preparation room, which was usually adjacent to the computer. With developments in computer communications, it is no longer necessary to locate terminals or other input/output devices near the computer.

A terminal can be linked to a computer system over ordinary telephone lines. To do this, the electronic (digital) signals to and from the computer equipment have to be converted into audio signals. The process of conversion into audio signals is called *modulation* and the conversion back into digital signals is called *demodulation*. The device that is connected between the telephone line and the computer to perform this task is called a *modem* (modulator–demodulator). There has to be a modem at the computer end and at the terminal end of the telephone line.

The modem may be wired permanently into a telephone line, but alternatively it is possible to use a normal telephone receiver in conjunction with a small device called an *acoustic coupler*. An acoustic coupler has moulded rubber sockets forming a soundproof container into which the telephone handset is inserted. The output from the terminal's modem is a series of audio tones which is picked up by the telephone mouthpiece. The output from the computer's modem generates audio tones at the earpiece. A microphone at the earpiece feeds these tones into the modem. The advantage of an acoustic coupler is that no direct wiring is needed between the terminal and the computer, and as telephone lines are used, the coupler can be used wherever there is a telephone.

An acoustic coupler, keyboard and printer can be built into a briefcase. This briefcase can then be connected via an ordinary telephone to any computer in the world that will accept the user. The user dials the computer's telephone number and the computer responds by requesting that the user identifies himself by inputting an account number and password. When you communicate with a computer elsewhere in the world, the link may also involve the use of a satellite to transmit the signals for part of the distance.

It is possible to have a very compact terminal that communicates over the telephone (see Figure 1.12). This is a data entry terminal and it is about the size of a pocket calculator. During the course of a day, a salesman, say, can enter the orders he takes into the terminal's memory. When he gets home, he can plug the terminal into a telephone receiver mouthpiece, dial the computer's telephone number, and transmit all his orders into his company's main computer.

Another communications development is the linking together on one site of several microcomputers into a local area network

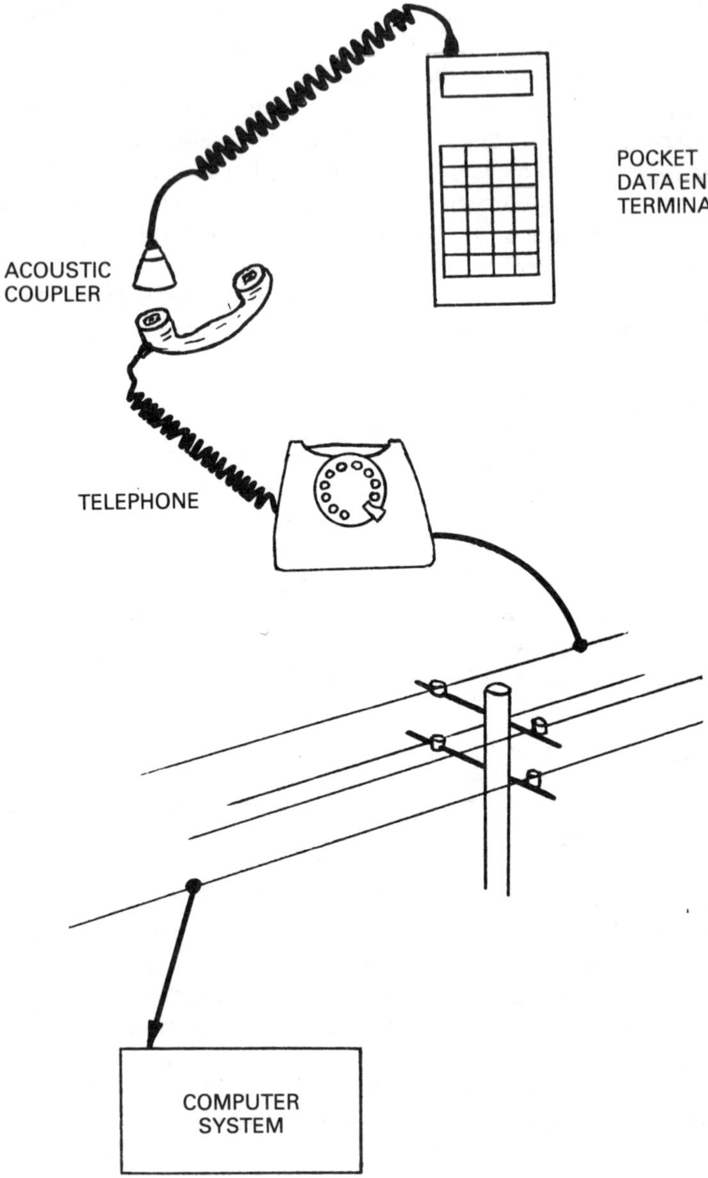

POCKET
DATA ENTRY
TERMINAL

ACOUSTIC
COUPLER

TELEPHONE

COMPUTER
SYSTEM

Figure 1.12 A pocket data entry terminal

(LAN). As well as being able to share common printers and disk units attached to the LAN, users can send messages to each other on their microcomputers through the network using special software. This facility is known as electronic mail.

2

Computer Software

Overview

Several different types of software (computer programs) are needed when using computers. These include an operating system (controlling program), which may be specific to a particular range of machines or a 'standard' that can be used with different machines.

Many different programming languages can be used, each needing a translator program (interpreter or compiler) to convert the instructions, written in a particular programming language, into the computer's own machine code.

Software packages for a variety of applications – scientific and commercial – allow computers to be used without writing new programs. Similarly, common routine tasks, necessary for running a computer system, are carried out using commercially-available utility programs. A large amount of software is available commercially and some may be supplied free when buying a computer. Good documentation for all software is essential (see page 47).

Operating systems

A computer will only function if it has a controlling program in its memory. This program is called an *operating system* and may be held in ROM chips inside the computer.

The purpose of the operating system is to provide the basic instructions to the central processor so that the various units which make up the computer system function as intended. The operating system interprets commands entered by users, sends messages to users, and controls the peripheral devices, such as printers and disk units, which are attached to the central processor.

In time-sharing installations, where many terminal users share the central processor and peripheral facilities, the operating system supervises the input/output activity throughout the system and logs the use of the various terminals and peripherals. The log may be stored on disk for later analysis and accounting purposes. In addition, such an operating system will have facilities for checking user codes and passwords so as to prevent unauthorised access to the computer system. Security aspects are discussed further in Chapter 10.

Even a stand-alone (single-user) microcomputer needs a simple operating system for saving, loading and running programs, and communicating with the user. This is illustrated at the end of the chapter.

A program recorded under one operating system cannot be used with a different operating system. This has led to the development of 'standard' operating systems, particularly for business micro-computers. Examples are CP/M (Digital Research's Control Program for microcomputers – there are versions for 8-bit and 16-bit microprocessors), MSDOS (Microsoft's Disk Operating System), PCDOS (IBM's Personal Computer Disk Operating System), and UNIX (Bell Laboratories' universal operating system available on small and large computers).

Programming languages

Computers are constructed so that they understand a fixed set of binary instructions called *machine code*. Writing in binary is very tedious and exacting, and can lead to many errors. To make the process easier, programs can be written in other codes called *programming languages*. The computer itself automatically converts the program from the language into machine code using translator programs which have to be in main storage during the translation process.

A range of languages is available to the programmer. Those that make use of mnemonic codes or binary digits are called *low-level* languages, while those that use English words and mathematical symbols are called *high-level* languages.

Low-level languages are translated into machine code by a program called an assembler on an instruction-for-instruction basis. At the same time, the assembler program can output information to indicate errors in the way the language has been used to write the program.

An instruction in a high-level language is usually equivalent to several instructions in machine code. High-level languages can be translated into machine code by two types of program – *interpreters* or *compilers*.

Interpreters translate one instruction at a time when the program is being used. The interpreter waits for the computer to execute the translated instruction before going on to the next instruction. This means that any errors in the use of the original programming language (known as *syntax errors*) are not discovered until part way through a run.

A compiler translates the original program completely before it is executed. During this process of compilation, any syntax errors that are found are listed on a screen or by a printer. The original program (source program) is amended as many times as required until there are no syntax errors. The compiled (machine code) version is then retained for subsequent use. If the program needs to be corrected, the changes are made to the source program and the whole program is recompiled.

Most personal microcomputers use an interpreter (which may be contained in a ROM chip) so that you can use the specified high-level language in an easy fashion. Compilers are used in large-scale applications where the time taken to develop a satisfactory compiled program is offset by the advantages of having a compiled program for, say, daily use. In general, a compiled program, having been translated into machine code, runs faster than a program that has to be interpreted into machine code every time it is used.

Different high-level programming languages have been designed for particular types of application. BASIC was designed for teaching programming to beginners. It is available on most microcomputers and has been extended so that it can be used for many different applications. COBOL (COmmercial Business Oriented Language) is used for commercial applications and has been designed for file handling. FORTRAN (FORmula TRANslator) is used for mathematical/scientific work. Another high-level programming language, Pascal, makes it easier to structure programs in a clear way for any application. Programming languages and techniques are discussed further in Chapter 3.

Software packages and utility programs

A *software package* is a group, or suite, of programs written for a particular type of application, for example, a pay-roll, stock control, accounting or word processing application.

The development of standard operating systems has resulted in companies (software houses) specialising in the production of software packages for running under one or more of the widely used operating systems. Many thousands of packages are available for scientific and commercial use. Prices vary from less than a hundred pounds to several thousand pounds, depending on the complexity of the package and its universal appeal.

The user may have considerable flexibility when using the package by selecting options. An important consideration is the ease of use of the package through the availability of menus (lists of options displayed on the computer's screen) and help messages, and this is discussed further in Chapter 4.

Using a software package eliminates the program-writing and program-testing stages of developing a system. A good software package will show considerable savings in costs and time. However, it is still necessary to test the system with sample data, to carry out the conversion of manual files to computer files, training and office planning. Some programs may need to be written and linked to the package's routines to provide the required system.

It is important to ensure that very good documentation is supplied with the package, as often it is not possible to refer back to the originators of the software. The user manual should contain as a minimum:

A description of the computer configuration required;
A resumé of the methods used (for example, the particular techniques used in a forecasting package);
Input format details;
Output options;
Operating instructions;

Error messages with full explanations;
Examples of input and output.

In writing programs for computers and running a computer system, there is often the need to perform certain tasks almost as a matter of routine. For example, it will regularly be necessary to copy the information on a disk onto another disk or tape to provide a back-up copy, in case the original disk becomes damaged or the information becomes altered by faulty hardware or software. There may be a need to perform checks on the operation of the computer system, for example to test that all the memory cells in a RAM chip are retaining information correctly. Programs that are written and used for these types of routine checks are called *utility programs* or *utilities*, as they help in the use of the system.

In the early days of commercial computers, the software (operating system, utility or housekeeping programs, compilers, and some application programs) was supplied free with the computer system by the manufacturer. In the 1970s, manufacturers started to 'unbundle' their software from the hardware, and limited what was supplied to the operating system, some utility programs and one or two compilers. The rest of the software had to be purchased separately from the manufacturer or software houses.

In recent years, the cost of developing software has increased rapidly while the cost of hardware has dropped. The effect of this has been to move towards software packages, as described earlier in this chapter. Some business microcomputers are sold with a selection of useful software, for example, for word processing, financial modelling, file handling, different programming languages and utilities.

Running a BASIC program

We will use a simple program to illustrate how the user interacts with a microcomputer. The program is written in BASIC and is shown in Figure 2.1. The program is used to calculate a weekly milk bill, so we will give it the name 'BILL'. Note that the instructions are for a particular range of microcomputers, and may vary according to the computer used.

The first stage is to key the program into the computer as

```
10 INPUT "PINTS OF MILK";M
20 INPUT "COST PER PINT";MP
30 T=M*MP
40 INPUT "LOAVES OF BREAD";B
50 INPUT "COST PER LOAF";BP
60 T=T+B*BP
70 INPUT "CARTONS OF YOGHURT";Y
80 INPUT "COST PER CARTON";YP
90 T=T+Y*YP
100 PRINT
110 PRINT "TOTAL COST = £";T/100
120 PRINT "————————————————————————"
130 END
```

Figure 2.1 Listing of 'BILL' program

described in Chapter 1. The computer will start executing the program from line 10 when the operating system command RUN is entered, and

PINTS OF MILK?

will be displayed on the screen. The number of pints of milk bought that week (say, 14) is keyed in, and the RETURN key is pressed. This will cause the number 14 to be stored in a memory cell called M (see line 10). M is known as a *variable* or *variable name*, because on another occasion we may key in 12 instead of 14. Thus the contents of memory cells (also known as *locations*) can vary during a run of a program or from one run to another. For example, in line 30, the variable T will contain the result of multiplying ($*$ means multiply) the contents of location M (i.e. 14) by the contents of location MP (say, 21). This means that after line 30 has been executed, T will contain $14 \times 21 = 294$. However, the contents of T will change later in the program, after lines 60 and 90 have been executed. Further data is entered at lines 40, 50, 70 and 80 (say, 4, 45, 6, 18 for B, BP, Y and YP respectively).

After line 60 has been executed, T will contain its last value (294) plus 4×45 (180), that is, $294 + 180 = 474$. Similarly, after line 90 has been executed, T will contain 474 plus 6×18, that is, 582. Line 110 completes the calculation by dividing (/ means divide) to give £5.82 as the total cost. Line 120 underlines the result with dashes.

Further operating system commands can now be used to record (save) the program on a cassette tape. The command SAVE followed by the program name is used as shown in Figure 2.2. The computer tells us to press the *record* and *play* buttons on the cassette recorder. The program will be recorded on the tape preceded by a 'header' containing the program name (BILL) so it can be found at a later stage for loading back into the computer's memory. The computer displays READY when the recording is finished.

```
SAVE "BILL"
PRESS RECORD AND PLAY ON TAPE
OK
SAVING
READY
VERIFY "BILL"
PRESS PLAY ON TAPE
OK
SEARCHING
FOUND BILL
VERIFYING
OK
READY
▧
```

Figure 2.2 SAVE and VERIFY commands

Something may have gone wrong with the recording, so it is a good idea to verify the finished recording. The tape is first rewound to the beginning of the recorded program (using the counter on the cassette recorder to make sure the tape position is correct) prior to verifying the recording. This is initiated by the operating system command VERIFY which will cause the recorded program to be compared with that held in the computer's memory. If they are both the same, then OK is output. The tape is only read during verification hence only the play button is pressed on the recorder.

We may want to change the program to give totals for each of four weeks and the month. The additional and changed BASIC instructions required are shown in Figure 2.3. The FOR . . . NEXT instructions at lines 5 and 124 cause all the instructions between these lines to be repeated four times (for the four weeks of the month). The weekly totals are added each time to a monthly total

```
LOAD "BILL"
PRESS PLAY ON TAPE
OK
SEARCHING
FOUND BILL
LOADING
READY
3 TM=0
5 FOR I=1 TO 4
95 TM=TM+T
110 PRINT "TOTAL FOR WEEK";I;"=£";T/100
120 PRINT "_____"
122 PRINT
124 NEXT I
126 PRINT
128 PRINT "TOTAL FOR MONTH = £";TM/100
129 PRINT "*************************"
■
```

Figure 2.3   Amendments to 'BILL' program

held in the variable TM, which is set to zero at line 3, and finally output at line 128.

Notice the operating system command LOAD at the beginning. This asks the computer to find the program 'BILL' on tape and to load it into the memory so that it can be amended, by keying in the new and changed instructions. A complete listing of the instructions in the revised program can be obtained by the operating system command LIST, for checking purposes.

After the program has been run again, the calculated totals for the sample data will appear on the screen, as shown in Figure 2.4.

Week Number	1	2	3	4
Pints of milk	14	17	15	20
Cost per pint	21	21	21	20
Loaves of bread	4	6	5	6
Cost per loaf	45	44	45	46
Cartons of yoghurt	6	8	5	9
Cost per carton	18	17	19	18
Weekly totals	£5.82	£7.57	£6.35	£8.38
Total for month	£28.12			

Figure 2.4   Sample data and expected results

Part of program development is concerned with testing with sample data and checking the results by performing the calculations (using a pocket calculator if necessary). Once a program has been thoroughly tested, it can be used many times with different data.

3

Programming Languages and Techniques

Overview

Many different programming languages have been designed for different purposes. Some of these were invented many years ago; recent implementations have features that enable them to be used with modern programming techniques.

Languages such as BASIC, COBOL and Pascal are available on large and small computers. However, the microcomputer implementations exploit the interactive features of these machines, and allow input/output ports to be accessed for communicating with peripherals and for controlling equipment.

Commercial and industrial applications are designed, in many cases, by a team of systems analysts and programmers. The programs need to be documented clearly so that, at a later stage, the same or different programmers can amend the programs to allow for new conditions.

A modern programming technique is used to make programs more readable. This involves structuring the program to show the logic clearly. Programs can be structured in this way using any programming language. However, the task is made easier if the language has been designed around these concepts, like Pascal, or if special types of instruction are available, as in FORTRAN 77.

An older technique uses diagrammatic representations of the logic called *flowcharts*. This method is suitable for small programs. Larger programs may be divided up into small sections (modules); this technique is known as *modular programming*. An advantage of this method is that each module can be written and tested separately as a *subroutine* or *subprogram*, and linked together into a large application program at a later stage. Subroutines contain sets of instructions that may be used more than once in the program or in different programs, and so their use saves time in writing and testing programs.

BASIC is widely used in schools and with home computers. However, some other languages have also been introduced into schools. One of these is COMAL (COMmon Algorithmic Language) which has structured facilities similar to Pascal, but otherwise is more like BASIC. Since the introduction of COMAL, several versions of BASIC have structured facilities, including the latest version of Microsoft BASIC and BBC BASIC.

Other programming languages used in education are LOGO and PILOT, which have quite different purposes. LOGO allows even young children to program a microcomputer quickly, to draw pictures, for example. PILOT is an 'author' language that can be used by teachers and trainers to write programs for Computer Assisted Learning (CAL).

These and other educational applications, including those involving colour graphics, sound and control of equipment, are described in Chapter 9.

The US Department of Defense has funded a project to promote the portability of software which can easily be maintained. As much as seventy per cent of total programming time can be spent on maintenance and upgrading of software if there is a lack of standardisation of languages and poor programming techniques are used. This project has resulted in the design of another language called Ada, which is partly based on Pascal. The aim of Ada is to provide a standard language suitable for programming real time systems, which control sophisticated equipment, for example, and systems which have complex calculations and data structures. Readability of programs and reliability are key issues in the design of Ada. Full Ada compilers are large, typically with 100000 lines of code.

A completely different concept in programming is called object oriented programming. This deals with objects and messages, rather than distinguishing between data and processing, as in the more traditional languages such as BASIC, COBOL, etc. A typical application, where object oriented programming is used, is for handling the advanced type of work station display described in

Chapter 4. A language for object oriented programming, called Smalltalk-80, was devised by the Learning Research Group at Xerox Research in the USA.

Developing a program

This development of a program goes through several stages, whether the application is a large commercial one or a small program for a microcomputer.

Before any programming is undertaken, the system needs to be analysed and designed. It may take a team of computer professionals many months to analyse, design and program a commercial application. The development of a small system on a microcomputer can also benefit from a planned approach, as illustrated in the following simple example.

The first step is to analyse the user's requirements, that is, to write down everything that needs to be considered to form a specification. This information will include:

The purpose of the program;
Details of the data it will use;
Details of any calculations to be carried out;
The way the results are to be presented.

Documentation should start with this specification and be added to as the application is developed. To illustrate the above ideas, the development of a simple program will be described.

Firstly, the purpose of the program is to provide information on repaying a loan. The data to be used will be entered at the keyboard, and will consist of:

1   The size of the loan;
2   The interest rate;
3   The loan period.

This data will be entered in response to prompts on the screen, as shown in Figure 3.1. The user needs to agree the data is correct before the calculation stage is entered. If the data is incorrect, due to mis-typing or a change of mind, the prompts will be repeated, and the data can be entered again.

```
LOAN-CALC: DATA ENTRY
*********************

SIZE OF LOAN          ?  10000

INTEREST RATE (%) ?  12.5

LOAN PERIOD           ?  25


CORRECT (Y/N) ?  Y
```
Figure 3.1   Data entry stage

It is required to calculate the repayments, on a monthly and on a yearly basis. In addition, it is required to calculate a table showing the allocation of the repayments to interest and capital on a yearly basis for the duration of the loan. The calculations are to be based on a yearly compounding of interest. Monthly payments by the borrower are just regarded as a convenient way of accumulating the annual repayment.

The results are obtained in two stages. Firstly, the calculated monthly and yearly repayments will be displayed as shown in Figure 3.2. Users can then select one of three options. They can change the data, proceed to viewing a repayments table or quit the program. The repayments table is arranged as shown in Figure 3.3. Because the number of lines on a screen is limited, the table displays fifteen repayment periods at a time. The user is required to 'PRESS A KEY TO CONTINUE' to the next page.

```
LOAN-CALC: RESULTS
*****************

REPAYMENTS : MONTHLY 109.95
           : YEARLY  1319.43

CHANGE DATA, VIEW TABLE, QUIT C/V/Q? V

PRESS A KEY TO CONTINUE
```
Figure 3.2   Repayments display

```
PRESS A KEY TO CONTINUE
*****************************************
```

PER	PAYMENT	INTEREST PAID	LOAN REPAID	BAL
1	1319.43	1250.00	69.43	9930.57
2	1319.43	1241.32	78.11	9852.45
3	1319.43	1231.56	87.88	9764.57
4	1319.43	1220.57	98.86	9665.71
5	1319.43	1208.21	111.22	9554.49
6	1319.43	1194.31	125.12	9429.37
7	1319.43	1178.67	140.76	9288.60
8	1319.43	1161.08	158.36	9130.25
9	1319.43	1141.28	178.15	8952.09
10	1319.43	1119.01	200.42	8751.67
11	1319.43	1093.96	225.48	8526.19
12	1319.43	1065.77	253.66	8272.53
13	1319.43	1034.07	285.37	7987.16
14	1319.43	998.40	321.04	7666.13
15	1319.43	958.27	361.17	7304.96

```
PRESS A KEY TO CONTINUE


*****************************************
```

PER	PAYMENT	INTEREST PAID	LOAN REPAID	BAL
16	1319.43	913.12	406.31	6898.64
17	1319.43	862.33	457.10	6441.54
18	1319.43	805.19	514.24	5927.30
19	1319.43	740.91	578.52	5348.77
20	1319.43	668.60	650.84	4697.94
21	1319.43	587.24	732.19	3965.74
22	1319.43	495.72	823.72	3142.03
23	1319.43	392.75	926.68	2215.35
24	1319.43	276.92	1042.52	1172.83
25	1319.43	146.60	1172.83	0. 0

```
*****************************************
```

Figure 3.3   Repayments table

The above outline of the objectives and requirements of the program form the basis on which the task of programming can be undertaken. However, before writing a program in a programming language, it is necessary to determine the required sequence of instructions. A logical sequence for this example is shown in Figure 3.4, in the form of a flowchart. This chart uses the special symbols explained in Figure 3.5. Next a detailed flowchart is prepared.

Once the flowchart has been prepared, the task of writing the computer program can begin. The program in this case has been written in BASIC and is shown in Figure 3.6.

The Data Entry Stage, as shown on the flowchart, results in the writing of program lines 100 to 180. This stage is indicated by a REM (REMark) statement in line 100. A main heading is PRINTed out in line 110 and then lines 140, 160 and 180 accept INPUTed values from the keyboard in response to the respective prompt messages. Lines containing solely a PRINT statement, 105, 107, 130, etc., print a blank line on the screen, thereby spacing out the heading and the prompts. At this stage the size of the loan, the interest rate and the loan period are stored in variables L, I and N respectively.

The next stage indicated in the flowchart is to check that the data is acceptable to the user. This is done in the program over lines 190 to 230. Lines 190 and 200 space the question in line 210 further down the screen. The user's response Y or N (Yes, the data is correct, or No, the data is not correct) is stored in the variable A$. The user's response is tested in line 230, so if N was input at line 210, then the computer branches back to line 110, and requests the data again. Otherwise the computer continues to line 300.

When the data is accepted as correct by the user, the repayment calculations are made over lines 300 to 340. Line 310 defines a function FNM that will round values to two decimal places. This function is used several times in later instructions. The interest rate, entered as a percentage (e.g. 12), is converted to a decimal factor (e.g. 0.12) in line 320. The calculation of the repayment is carried out in two parts. First an intermediate result, the variable V, is calculated in line 330 and then used together with the variables L and I in line 340 to obtain the annual repayment, R.

The result is displayed, together with suitable headings, by lines 400 to 520. Line 510 prints the monthly repayments (by dividing R

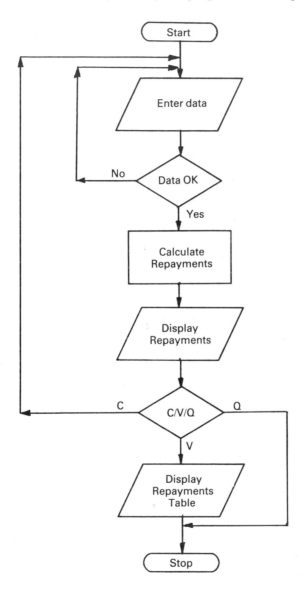

Figure 3.4 Flowchart of Loan Repayments

SYMBOL   USE

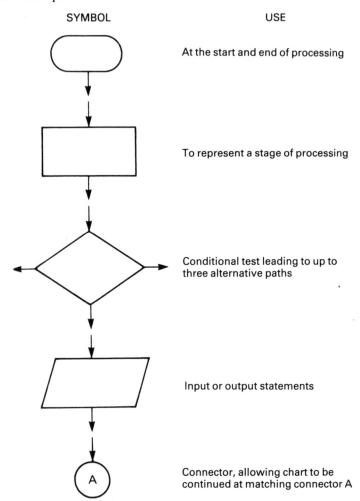

At the start and end of processing

To represent a stage of processing

Conditional test leading to up to
three alternative paths

Input or output statements

Connector, allowing chart to be
continued at matching connector A

Figure 3.5   Some flowchart symbols

by 12 and using the function FNM to round the answer to two
decimals), and line 520 prints the annual repayments.

At this stage the user is given the option, by lines 540 to 570, of
changing the data, viewing the repayments tables or quitting the
program. If the user responds to the message printed by line 540
with a 'C', then the computer returns to line 105 to recommence the

```
100 REM ***DATA INPUT STAGE***
105 PRINT
107 PRINT
110 PRINT "LOAN-CALC: DATA ENTRY"
120 PRINT "********************"
130 PRINT
140 INPUT "SIZE OF LOAN       ";L
150 PRINT
160 INPUT "INTEREST RATE (%) ";I
170 PRINT
180 INPUT "LOAN PERIOD       ";N
190 PRINT
200 PRINT
210 INPUT "CORRECT (Y/N) ";A$
220 PRINT
230 IF A$= "N" THEN 110
300 REM ***CALCULATION STAGE***
310 DEF FNM(Z)=INT(Z/.01+.5)*.01
320 I=I/100
330 V=(1+I)^N
340 R=L*I*V/(V-1)
400 REM ***DISPLAY RESULTS***
410 PRINT "LOAN-CALC: RESULTS"
420 PRINT "******************"
500 PRINT
510 PRINT "REPAYMENTS : MONTHLY";FNM(R/12)
520 PRINT "           : YEARLY ";FNM(R)
530 PRINT
540 PRINT "CHANGE DATA, VIEW TABLE, QUIT C/V/Q";
550 INPUT A$
560 IF A$="C" THEN 105
570 IF A$<>"V" THEN STOP
```

Figure 3.6a   Loan repayments program

data entry stage. If the user's response is not a 'C' then line 570 tests for a 'V'. If the response was not a 'V' then the program STOPs at line 570, otherwise it continues to line 600 (see overleaf).

Lines 600 to 720 comprise the routine to produce the repayments table. The reducing capital balance (variable B) is set initially to L in line 610. Line 620 sets up a blank string in S$ that will be used to format the output neatly. A loop count is set up over lines 630 to 710 to produce repayment details for each period from period 1 to period N. Line 640 performs a calculation so that at every 15th period the computer will jump to the subroutine starting at line 800 (this subroutine produces the repayments table heading).

```
600 REM ***REPAYMENTS TABLE***
610 B=L
620 S$="              "
630 FOR J= 1 TO N
640 IF(J-1)/15 = INT((J-1)/15) THEN GOSUB 800.
650 C=I*B:D=R-C:B=B-D
660 J$=RIGHT$(S$+STR$(J),3)
665 AM=R:GOSUB 900:R$=M$
670 AM=C:GOSUB 900:C$=M$
680 AM=D:GOSUB 900:D$=M$
690 AM=B:GOSUB 900:B$=M$
700 PRINT J$+R$+C$+D$+B$
710 NEXT J
715 PRINT"**************************************"
720 STOP
800 REM *** TABLE HEADING SUBROUTINE ***
810 PRINT
820 PRINT "PRESS A KEY TO CONTINUE"
825 GET K$:IFK$=""THEN 825
830 PRINT"**************************************"
840 PRINT
850 PRINT"PER  PAYMENT  INTEREST   LOAN     BAL"
860 PRINT"                   PAID    REPAID
870 PRINT"**************************************"
880 RETURN
900 REM ***LINE UP DECIMAL***
910 M$=STR$(INT(AM))
920 W=INT(100*AM+.5)
930 W$=RIGHT$(STR$(W),2)
940 IF AM=0 THEN W$="00"
950 M$=M$+"."+W$
960 M$=RIGHT$(S$+M$,9)
970 RETURN
```

Figure 3.6b   Loan repayments program (contd)

The values to be printed in the repayments table are calculated in line 650. The interest charge, C, is calculated, then from this the amount remaining out of the repayment, $R - C$, is calculated as the depreciation on the balance (D). Lastly, the revised balance is calculated ($B - D$).

Lines 660 to 690 format the 'answers' neatly before they are printed in line 700. The string variable J$ is a formatted version of the period number J. The value of J is converted to a string and preceded by blanks (i.e. S$), the righthand three characters are then selected for storing in J$. This has the effect of formatting the period value to a width of three characters.

A similar approach is adopted with the other values that are output, but because it is necessary with monetary amounts to ensure that zero decimal values are printed, the formatting uses a subroutine (lines 900 to 970). Using a common subroutine means that each variable in turn (for example, R, see line 665) has to be copied into a common variable (AM) before the subroutine is called. When the program returns from the subroutine, the formatted result, stored in M$, has then to be copied to a suitable string variable, R$. This procedure is repeated for each variable over lines 665 to 690. A complete line of formatted output is then printed by line 700.

When the program has executed the FOR . . . NEXT loop N times, line 715 prints a final underlining to the table. The program finally stops at line 720.

Program testing

This example shows how a program is developed using a flowchart and then coded in a particular programming language. It is important to check the logic of the flowchart by going through it with suitable test data. Every part of the flowchart needs to be tested by going through each 'path'. Once the flowchart has been checked, and corrected if necessary, the program can be coded in the chosen programming language.

Program testing involves a number of different steps. The manual checking of the code with test data, known as *dry-running*, may show up some errors in coding. For example, the command PRINT may have been misspelt as PRNT or some of the punctuation may be incorrect (either missing or inserted in the wrong place). This type of mistake, in the way the programming language is used, is known as a *syntax error*. Any syntax errors prevent the computer from interpreting that particular instruction, so these must be corrected before the program can be executed by the computer.

The first checking of the code should take place after the program has been written down. As well as finding some syntax errors, the logic is tested again to match the flowchart. The expected results for the test data will need to be calculated, using a pocket calculator if necessary, and checked against the results obtained by tracing through the flowchart and program code.

Next, the program code is keyed into the computer's memory from the keyboard. The BASIC interpreter may do some syntax checking at this stage, and will display an error message for any wrong instruction so that it can be corrected. Some errors may not be detected until the program is run. An execution error may occur during the running of a program. For example, if a value is divided by zero (because of an error in the logic of the program), then the effect is to make the answer infinity, which obviously cannot be stored in a memory location. The computer can only store numbers within its range, so any attempt to store a number which is too large or too small will cause an execution error.

Another type of execution error will occur if an attempt is made to enter non-numeric (alphanumeric) data into a variable assigned as numeric, since the two types of data are stored in different ways in the computer's memory. Any execution error causes the computer to stop executing the program, and to display an error message.

A program that runs without causing an execution error may still not be correct, since the results may be wrong, or the output may not be that specified in the system requirements. Careful checking of the logic in the flowchart and coding stages against the expected results, should eliminate most if not all of the logic errors, provided the test data has been chosen to test every part of the program. This is more difficult in a large program where the links between different modules also have to be tested carefully. Testing can take a long time but is an essential procedure for successful results.

Note

There are some differences in the way BASIC is implemented on various computers. However, much of the language is standard and this has been selected for the range of simple mathematical, scientific and business applications given in *Computer Programming in BASIC* (Teach Yourself Books), by the present authors. These programs and some additional ones, including the file processing and reporting example given in Chapter 5, have been implemented using the facilities available on a *specific* microcomputer in *Computer Programming with the Commodore 64* (Teach Yourself Books), also by the present authors.

Documentation

The documentation required will depend on the type and size of system. Most companies will have standards which need to be adhered to. The National Computing Centre publishes details of documentation standards. Appropriate documentation is likely to contain the following sections.

Identification   Title page showing unique name of program or subroutine, programmer's name and location, date of completion. The computer configuration can be included here or in the summary below.

Contents page   Section names with page numbers.

Summary   Functions and limitations of programs.

Description of problem   Background information, formulae, references to tables (held in appendices).

Specification of program   In words and diagrams (e.g. flowcharts). This must be up-to-date to match the final program code (listed in an appendix).

Input and output formats   Details of all input and output data, layouts for screen displays and printed output.

Use of program   Method for inputting data, loading and running instructions for the program (operating instructions).

Interpretation of outputs   Details to enable users to understand the functions of the program fully.

Modifications   Changes to the program (flowchart, logic description, coding) because the system has been revised. New test data may need to be included.

Appendices   Detailed information referred to in the text.

Structured programming

In the early days of computing, programs were mainly written by mathematicians, scientists and engineers who used machine code or FORTRAN. Later BASIC was used for teaching programming and COBOL for commercial programming, with some routines written in an assembly language, particularly for input and output procedures.

At that time the equipment was much less powerful and relatively more expensive than it is today. Subsequently, as computers became more widely used, the shortage of experienced computer professionals led to high salaries and frequent changes of employment by programmers.

When programmers left, it was sometimes necessary for companies to employ people with limited professional training in programming techniques, and the programs left behind were not always properly tested and documented. There was a great need for a more professional approach to programming, from design, through coding and testing to implementation.

An early approach was to divide the programs up into modules. Modular programming is now an established successful technique for producing large programs which are fully tested. A newer approach is that of structured programming. Techniques have been invented for ensuring that the data and the associated program are structured in such a way as to make the program easy to understand by any programmer who may be faced with having to amend it, due to changing circumstances. In addition, good program design, which increases the clarity of the program, helps to achieve correct results more quickly.

Pascal

A good structured design is achievable with any programming language; however, some languages have special facilities for structuring programs. One such language is called Pascal. This has been implemented on large computers and on some microcomputers. The language is more complex than BASIC and takes longer to learn. It is often used in universities and colleges for teaching programming to students since it instills good programming techniques and can be used for all types of application.

Figure 3.7 shows a program written in Pascal. The program calculates values of y for different values of x given that:

$$y = 261.378 \text{ times } \sqrt{1 + x^2}$$

and x has the values 1.00, 1.01, 1.02 . . . 3.00, that is, 300 values. Each pair of x,y values is printed out on a separate line to form a table.

```
PROGRAM table ( output );
CONST factor  = 261.378;
      hundred = 100.0;
VAR   x,
      y     : real;
      step  : integer;
BEGIN
   FOR step := 100 TO 300 DO
      BEGIN
        x := step / hundred;
        y := factor * sqrt ( 1.0 + sqr(x));
        writeln ( x, y )
      END
END.
```

Figure 3.7   A Pascal program

At the beginning of the Pascal program, two constants are named:

Factor = 261.378

and

hundred = 100.0

From then on, the names *factor* and *hundred* stand for the two values declared.

Next, three variables are given the types *real* (for *x* and *y*) and *integer* (for the name *step*). A real variable refers to numbers which have decimal places, while an integer variable refers to whole numbers only. If we try to store a 'real' number in a memory location referenced by an integer variable, this could result in decimal places being lost, and therefore this is not allowed.

The rest of the program is structured with three instructions. Two instructions calculate the value of *x* (as step divided by a hundred) and *y* as factor (i.e. 261.378) multiplied by the square root of $1 + x^2$. The third instruction prints the contents of memory locations *x* and *y* on a line (writeln). These three instructions are made into a 'compound statement' by preceding them with the word BEGIN and following them with the word END, so that all three instructions can be considered as a single instruction or statement. This compound statement is repeated for step values of 100,101, 102 up to 300, because of the FOR loop.

Loop control is also achieved in Pascal by other statements, apart from the FOR statement. For example, the word WHILE can be used instead of FOR, to indicate that a compound statement has to be repeated until a certain condition occurs. Alternatively, a set of statements can be REPEATed UNTIL a certain condition is true.

These types of statements are also used in versions of BASIC which have 'structured' facilities.

Programming systems software

Systems software, such as operating systems and compilers, used to be written mainly in assembly languages to give the programmer maximum control over the system. In addition, an assembly language or machine code program should be more 'efficient' than a high level language program which has been compiled. This is because the compilation process may produce a machine code program that runs more slowly and takes up more memory space than if it had been *written* at the 'machine-level'.

However, assembly programs take longer to develop, and are not easily understood by other programmers. This has led some computer manufacturers to use Pascal for their systems software, and also another programming language called C.

C

C was invented at Bell Laboratories and is a programming language with structured facilities, similar to Pascal. It also has some instructions that give control at the machine level. This allows programs to be written which are largely machine-independent.

The UNIX operating system, mentioned in Chapter 2, is itself written in C. It has over 250000 lines in C code with only a few hundred lines of machine code, making it readily transportable to different computers.

Versions of the UNIX system are available on several micro-computers, as well as on larger computer systems. UNIX is more than an operating system since users are provided with the C compiler and a range of software tools – for example, a program called Lint, which can be used by a programmer to tidy up a C program and to identify machine-independent code. Some application programs are also included, so that the operating system is a small percentage of the total software made available to UNIX users.

Some computer manufacturers have implemented C compilers to run under operating systems other than UNIX, one of the main incentives being the portability of C programs from one computer to another.

Commercial programming

COBOL

Most programs for commercial applications are written in COBOL. The first COBOL standard was issued by the American National Standards Institute (ANSI) in the 1960s. Revised ANSI COBOL standards are issued at intervals (every four to six years), after consultation with computer manufacturers and other organisations.

Although most companies providing COBOL compilers adhere fairly closely to the latest ANSI standard, they may not implement every feature, and may also introduce new features specific to their own equipment – for example, to handle the screen output of a particular microcomputer.

Whereas BASIC is generally written in free format, i.e. the various parts of an instruction do not start and end in particular column positions in a line, it is essential to write COBOL instructions in the correct columns. Special coding sheets are available which are divided up to show the sections used for different parts of the instructions.

A COBOL program contains four divisions. The first three divisions are descriptive and are used to identify the program (the identification division); to describe the computers used for compiling and running the program (the environment division), and to describe all the data areas including files and records to be used by the program (the data division). The fourth division contains the coded COBOL instructions for processing the data and producing reports, and is called the procedure division.

Figure 3.8 shows a small, complete COBOL program for displaying a total of all the salaries held on a number of different records in a 'salary' file.

You will notice that the COBOL instructions in the procedure division use English words instead of mathematical expressions.

```
        IDENTIFICATION DIVISION.
        PROGRAM-ID. SALT.
        AUTHOR. MELINDA FISHER.
    *       THIS PROGRAM ACCUMULATES SALARY DETAILS
        ENVIRONMENT DIVISION.
        CONFIGURATION SECTION.
        SOURCE-COMPUTER. ICL-2972.
        OBJECT-COMPUTER. ICL-2972.
        INPUT-OUTPUT SECTION.
        FILE-CONTROL.
            SELECT SALARY-FILE ASSIGN TO MS DA01.
        DATA DIVISION.
        FILE SECTION.
        FD SALARY-FILE.
        01 SALARY-RECORD.
            03 RECORD-TYPE                PIC X.
            03 SALARY                     PIC 9(6).
        WORKING-STORAGE SECTION.
        01 SALARY-TOTAL                   PIC 9(8).
        PROCEDURE DIVISION.
        AA-START.
            OPEN INPUT SALARY-FILE.
            MOVE ZEROS TO SALARY-TOTAL.
        BB-READ.
            READ SALARY-FILE AT END GO TO CC-END.
            ADD SALARY TO SALARY-TOTAL.
            GO TO BB-READ.
        CC-END.
            DISPLAY SALARY-TOTAL.
            CLOSE SALARY-FILE.
            STOP RUN.
```

Figure 3.8   A COBOL program

The procedure division is divided up into named paragraphs. The first instruction in the AA-START paragraph opens the SALARY-FILE for input, that is, information can be read from the file but not written to it. The file is assigned to a disk unit (MS), and given the name DA01, in the FILE-CONTROL paragraph of the environment division. The second instruction in AA-START puts zeros in a memory location which has the *data-name* (like a variable name in BASIC) SALARY-TOTAL.

The BB-READ paragraph reads a record from the SALARY-FILE. Each record contains just two items of data, a record type (one alphanumeric character, specified as PIC X) and a salary (six numeric digits specified as PIC 9(6)). PIC stands for picture, and describes each data item in a record or in a 'working-storage' field.

The second instruction, in BB-READ, adds the six-digit salary on the record just read to SALARY-TOTAL.

Records will continue to be read from the salary file, because of the GO TO BB-READ instruction, and their salary field contents added to SALARY-TOTAL until the end-of-file marker is reached, when the computer will start executing paragraph CC-END. The DISPLAY instruction will output the contents of the SALARY-TOTAL memory location. The file processing is then complete, so the SALARY-FILE is closed and the run is stopped.

A typical COBOL program as used in a large organisation could have thousands of instructions, divided up into small modules and each performing a special function. Generaly, a COBOL programmer works from a program specification giving details of the input processed and output required. In some installations, senior programmers design the programs, and junior programmers code and test the COBOL modules. The senior programmers, apart from supervising the coding, also become involved in the linking and testing of the modules, and finally in testing the complete program.

APL

As more managers are obtaining access to computers, there is a requirement for producing programs quickly when no suitable software package is available. APL (A Programming Language) may then be used for implementing a prototype system in a short time.

APL was invented by Ken Iverson, a Canadian mathematician, in the early 1960s. The language is very concise, and uses mathematical symbols to represent operations to be carried out on various types of data structures. Variable names and constants are used, but it is the ability to use special operators, for example, to handle tables, that makes APL so powerful. This means that a user can sit at a terminal or microcomputer, enter a single line of APL and immediately obtain the answer to a problem that would normally take several lines in BASIC or FORTRAN, for example.

If the prototype system, written in APL, is used frequently, it may be reprogrammed at a later stage in a different programming language to make it more efficient or comprehensive. For example, the APL program may be converted to COBOL for an application involving interrogation (making enquiries) of data files.

APL is used also by engineers and accountants for various types of calculations. However, an important growth in the use of APL is in the prototyping of systems required by managers who otherwise would have to wait many months for the data processing department to write the necessary COBOL programs

Scientific programming

One of the main languages used for writing programs that solve mathematical, scientific or engineering problems, is FORTRAN. This language is often taught to students studying these disciplines so that they can write their own programs.

Pascal and BASIC may also be used, but FORTRAN is popular because many mathematical routines, written in FORTRAN, are available in program libraries. These routines may be provided free by some manufacturers or software suppliers with the FORTRAN compiler, or a licence to use particular routines may be purchased.

FORTRAN 77

FORTRAN 77, the latest ANSI standard, has commands for handling characters and files so that it can be used for some data processing programs. There are also commands which allow structured programming techniques to be used.

The FORTRAN 77 program shown in Figure 3.9 is used to convert distances (in feet), read in and stored in a memory location called FEET, to distances in kilometres. Each converted distance is stored in a memory location called DIST and printed, together with the corresponding number of feet, after it has been calculated.

```
      PROGRAM CONVRT
      DO 10, N = 1, 5000
      READ *, FEET
      DIST = FEET / 3280.84
   10 PRINT *, FEET, DIST
      END
```

Figure 3.9   A FORTRAN program

The type of FORTRAN program required for complex scientific calculations, as used for example in astronomy, space exploration or nuclear physics, would make use of facilities such as built-in function (called *intrinsic functions* in FORTRAN) and subprograms from a standard program library.

Formulae can easily be translated into FORTRAN, for example:

$$t = 2\pi \sqrt{\frac{l}{g}}$$

represents the time (t) seconds of the swing of a simple pendulum, length (l) centimetres, when g is the gravitational constant. The equivalent FORTRAN statement, using T, L and G as the variables, is:

T = 2 * 3.14159 * SQRT(L/G)

where SQRT is an intrinsic function built into the FORTRAN compiler, and gives the square root of L divided by G; and * means multiply.

The result of the arithmetic expression on the righthand side of the equals sign is stored in memory location T, and could then be printed out using a PRINT statement.

Acknowledgments
The programs given in Figures 3.7, 3.8 and 3.9 are reproduced from the following Teach Yourself Books by permission of the authors:

Computer Programming in Pascal, by David Lightfoot;
Computer Programming in COBOL, by Melinda Fisher;
Computer Programming in FORTRAN, by Arthur Radford.

4

Communicating with Computers

Overview

One of the main changes in computing over the last few years has been in the way computers are used. Several methods have been developed for linking computers together in local area networks and over long distances using telephone lines and satellites. The company's digital switchboard, also known as a private automatic branch exchange (PABX), may be at the centre of the local communications system with links to other offices and also to public and private information systems. Videotex systems are available in many countries, to transmit 'pages' of information, as text or diagrams, from a remote computer, either over telephone lines (using the viewdata system), or broadcast by a television station (using the teletext system).

Figure 4.1 shows the way different types of equipment may be linked within an office. The equipment could include word-processing systems, local computer networks, videotex systems, and facsimile (FAX) equipment for world-wide transmission of 'images' of pages of text including pictures. OCR equipment may be used to read typed documents into word processors for subsequent amendment and printing, and computer information may be output onto microfilm or microfiche (COM) for permanent storage.

The aim is to provide business users with integrated systems to handle the processing of text, data, image, graphics and voice. This merging of computer, communications and associated technologies has been given the name Information Technology (IT).

Microcomputer-based work stations may be used by secretaries for word processing, and by managers for business planning, as described in Chapters 6 and 7. Further office automation facilities,

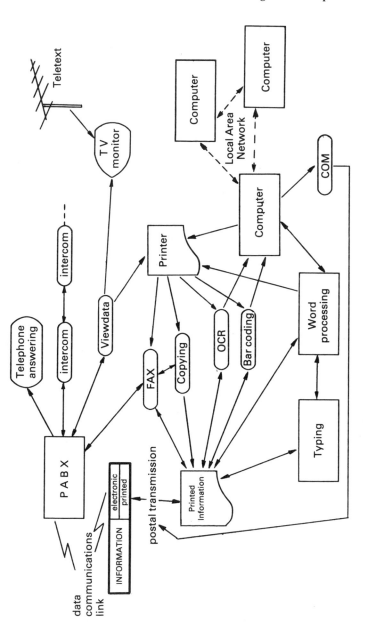

Figure 4.1 Information flow in an electronic office

such as electronic mail and appointments scheduling, may be provided on local area networks.

The hardware and software of the microcomputer work station are designed so as to provide a good man/machine interface, that is, to improve communications between the computer and the user.

Keyboards and visual display units

Using the work station keyboard is still the most common method of entering information into the computer, although alternative devices are available, as described later in the chapter.

The design of the keyboard is important as it can affect the user's accuracy when keying in information. The keyboard also needs to be comfortable to use. Most keyboard designs are based on the standard typewriter layout, known as QWERTY, because of the positions of these keys as the first sequence in the top row of the alphabetic keys. Additional keys are provided for special functions, such as delete, insert, and so on.

The numeric keys may be grouped in a keypad area like a calculator. This enables numeric data to be entered more quickly and accurately, using only one hand, than when the numbers are along the top row of the keyboard. In commercial computing, the bulk of the data input to computers is numeric.

The keys should have a positive feel, so that the user can feel when a key has been depressed. It is useful to have the keyboard separate from the visual display unit and linked by a flexible cable. This allows the user to place the keyboard in the most comfortable position.

There may be a choice of colour for the screen of the visual display unit or anti-dazzle colour filters may be used, such as green, blue, or amber. Both the keyboard and the VDU may be tiltable to give the best position for the lighting provided.

Prompts and help systems

Another aspect of the man/machine interface is concerned with the software, which should be designed to make the system easy to use.

Many systems are 'menu-driven'. That is, at each stage of the computer run, a list of options appears on the screen and the user can choose the required one, as shown in Figure 1.9, when a light pen was used for making selections.

Additionally, the software needs to prompt the user to enter the appropriate data by displaying a message on the screen. The response to the prompt should be tested by the software so that inappropriate responses are rejected, and the user is invited to enter a response again. For example, if information is to be stored on cassette tape or disk, the message.

STORE ON CASSETTE OR DISK C/D?

could be displayed. If neither C nor D is entered then the system should ask the question again rather than ignore the wrong response, otherwise the information would be lost instead of stored.

Help messages are useful, particularly for beginners. For example, a brief message may come up on the screen which is quite intelligible to the experienced user, but may mean nothing to a newcomer to the system. It is helpful if a further explanation can be obtained by pressing a key. If this fuller explanation was displayed each time, it would slow down the experienced user and also waste computer time.

Environmental conditions

Figure 4.2 shows the factors that affect the efficient/effective use of the equipment, known as *ergonomic* factors. Under adverse ergonomic conditions, the efficiency of the user diminishes and error rates are liable to rise.

Noise is particularly important in office environments where business matters need to be discussed and the telephone used. Noisy equipment such as printers can be put in specially-designed sound proof boxes, and this generally reduces the noise to a satisfactory level. The use of carpets, curtains and acoustic tiles can also reduce the noise level.

Suitable lighting is necessary so that the operator can view documents and also the screen without eye-strain. It is worth experimenting with the positions of the equipment and seating,

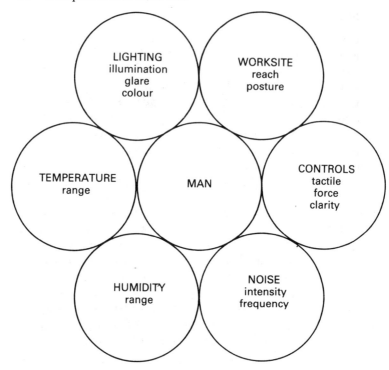

Figure 4.2   Ergonomic factors

since comfortable conditions may vary from one operator to another.

The type of computer equipment used in offices is designed to work in 'normal' temperature and humidity. However, if a lot of equipment is installed, it is advisable to consider installing some form of air-conditioning, mainly for the comfort of the users, although it may also prevent some overheating problems with equipment.

The controls, whether on the keyboard or on other parts of the equipment, need to be clearly marked and positive in their action without undue force being required. Warning messages should be displayed if some of the controls must only be adjusted by skilled operators. However, most of the adjustments on office equipment can easily be made by users after minimal training.

Videotex systems

These systems are classified as *non-interactive* or *broadcast* (teletext systems) or *interactive* (viewdata systems).

The two teletext systems available in the UK are: *Ceefax,* offered by the BBC, and *Oracle,* offered by the independent television companies. These teletext systems broadcast information on news items, the weather, sports, entertainment, etc. to every television receiver. To view the information, the receiver will need to contain special circuitry called a *teletext decoder.* The teletext decoder may be incorporated in the television set, or a separate adaptor may be purchased. The adaptor plugs into the aerial socket and the aerial is then plugged into the adaptor. Alternatively, microcomputers may have a teletext and viewdata decoder built in. A small keypad is used to key in the numbers listed in the main index alongside each entry to reach the item of information required.

The user of a viewdata system can communicate via the telephone system with the computer that holds the information. The system is interactive since the user communicates directly with the computer and the computer can respond immediately to the user. Companies can have their own in-house viewdata system on their computer. Such companies can then communicate information to their employees, who will be able to enter data, and access and process information held on the company's main computer files (the company data base), using adapted television sets or microcomputers as terminals.

Prestel

British Telecom runs a public viewdata system called Prestel. This enables anyone who is a registered user and has a Prestel receiver – for example, an adapted television set – to call up selected information on the television screen. This information is put on the Prestel system by Information Providers (IPs). These could be companies selling products, services or specialised information.

For example, a mail order company may hold its catalogue on Prestel. You could then browse through the menus by keying in the numbers listed on the index. If you select a product, you call up an order form on the screen, key in the details (perhaps your name, address and the products selected) using your keypad, and then send the order via Prestel by pressing the appropriate key on the keypad or microcomputer keyboard.

Directories are available which contain details of the services offered by Prestel Information Providers. The charges vary according to the type of service provided. A mail order company may not charge you for looking at its pages of information; advertisers also supply free information. However, a company selling, say, information on share prices or foreign currency exchange rates is likely to make a charge for every page of information viewed; the price is displayed on the page. Such up-to-date information on financial matters is very valuable to business users such as banks and stockbrokers.

Another use of viewdata is for transmitting computer programs, known as *telesoftware*. The programs can be 'downloaded' directly into the memory of a suitably adapted microcomputer. The user can then run the programs and also store them on cassette tape or disks for future use. Alternatively, teletext users can key the programs into their microcomputers as they are displayed on the computers' screens. The software may be developed by educational organisations or individual users, and made available free or at a low charge to schools, colleges and home users.

To use Prestel, an organisation or domestic user needs to be registered as a business or residential user of the Prestel system. Apart from the cost of the telephone call (usually at the local rate), there is a fixed quarterly charge for domestic and business users, and a Prestel computer time charge during peak periods only.

A Prestel jack socket needs to be attached to the telephone line and a lead from the television set or microcomputer is plugged into this. By pressing the appropriate key, the Prestel system is automatically dialled up and a connection is made to the Prestel computer. The telephone being used is engaged while using Prestel, and no incoming calls can be received during this period. At other times, the telephone can be used normally.

Pages of information are linked together on the Prestel system. If the number of a page is not known, this can be found from a routing page which will point to a 'lower-level' page. For example, you could look up Colleges of Higher Education to obtain a list of all colleges, and this page can then direct you to colleges in certain regions of the country. Finally, you may be directed to a particular college, and to pages of information for that college, such as the courses offered. However, if you know the number of the page required you can go directly to it.

Pages on the Prestel system are attractively displayed; words and diagrams can be coloured white, red, blue, green, yellow, cyan or magenta. These colours and black can also be set as background colours. The Prestel page has twenty-four rows of forty characters, any of which can be set to flash on and off to attract attention. Characters can also be set to double height for greater effect.

A demonstration videotex system

This example illustrates how a videotex system can be used to provide information. It is a simple system designed to be programmed in BASIC for implementation on a microcomputer, and to be used as a family videotex system.

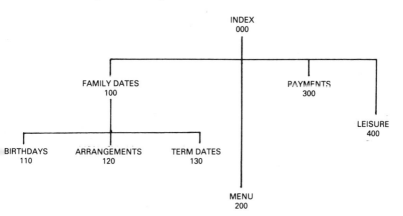

Figure 4.3 Structure of FAM-TEX pages

The structure of the 'FAM-TEX' pages is shown in Figure 4.3. Each page has a three-digit number which forms the basis of the indexing system. The first digit indicates the main heading under which the page is classified. For example, all pages beginning with 1 could be assigned to family dates. The second digit indicates a sub-division within the main heading, for example, 110 – birthdays, 120 – arrangements. The third digit is not used in this system, but

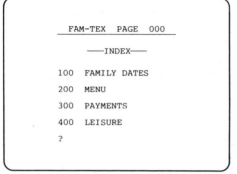

```
    FAM-TEX  PAGE  000

        ——INDEX——

    100  FAMILY DATES

    200  MENU

    300  PAYMENTS

    400  LEISURE

    ?
```

Figure 4.4   FAM-TEX menu

```
         FAM-TEX  PAGE  100



    110  BIRTHDAYS

    120  ARRANGEMENTS

    130  TERM DATES

    ?
```

Figure 4.5   Page 100 showing FAMILY DATES

```
    FAM-TEX  PAGE  120



    JULY   3   FETE

    JULY  24   JULIA'S

    AUG   12   DENTIST J.K.

    ?
```

Figure 4.6   Page 120 showing ARRANGEMENTS

has been included because three digits are commonly used in other systems.

A list of main headings can be obtained by viewing page 000. Keying in 000 will display the main menu, as shown in Figure 4.4. An option is selected by keying in the appropriate number. For example, entering 100 will select FAMILY DATES and cause a second menu to be displayed as shown in Figure 4.5; this shows the types of dates, that is, BIRTHDAYS, ARRANGEMENTS, TERM DATES.

To obtain further information about arrangements, 120 is entered and the information shown in Figure 4.6 is displayed. This display is not a menu, so there are no numbers against the lines of information. Entering any number, other than an existing page number, at this stage, displays the main menu again.

Further pages can be added by creating a new main heading, for example, PRESENT LISTS and given an index number 500. The index page 500 could show that 510, 520, 530, and so on, referred to lists of presents for different children in the family.

A system such as FAM-TEX demonstrates the principles of viewdata systems and at the same time can be fun for the family to use on a home microcomputer.

Advanced work stations

Much development work has been carried out on microcomputer-based work stations with the aim of providing managers with a tool that will increase their efficiency and reduce the amount of paper that is used.

Figure 4.7 shows the type of display available on advanced work stations. A section on the large screen is used to display pictures (icons) of typical office equipment, such as a calculator, a document folder, a waste paper basket, and a telephone.

Each icon represents a function that can be selected by moving the cursor (an arrow in this case) using a device called a 'mouse'. When the mouse is moved over the desk-top, the rotation of the mouse's track ball is detected by the computer and causes the cursor to move on the screen. Once the cursor is on the appropriate icon, a button on the mouse is pressed to select the required option; another button can be pressed to cancel the selection.

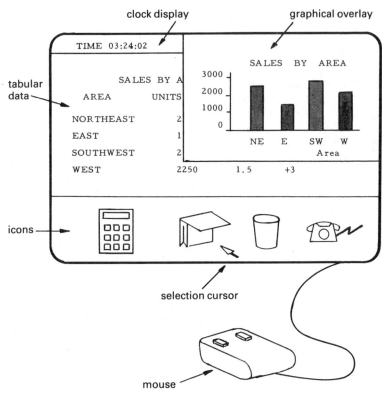

Figure 4.7   A work station

Documents can be selected from 'folders' and their contents displayed on the screen, and changed. They can then be put back in their folders by pointing to commands displayed on the screen when the folder function is selected. New documents or reports can be created using word processing facilities.

A report may need to contain the results of calculations, and the calculator function can be used to produce the calculations. Tabular information can be converted to graphs using other software in the system. The time-of-day is shown on the clock display, and this can be added to documents to indicate when they were created or updated. Documents that are no longer required can be 'thrown away' (deleted from the disk on which they were stored) by using the 'waste paper basket' function.

A feature of the display is the provision of multiple windows. That is, the screen can be divided up into a number of windows to display different types of information, such as the icons, clock, tabular data and graph as shown. In this case, the graph has been overlayed on top of the tabular data. When required, a command can be entered from the keyboard (not shown), or by moving the mouse to a particular function display, to bring the tabular data to the foreground.

The precise facilities available, their method of selection and displays, vary according to the work station used. However, hardware and software products are marketed which allow microcomputers to be converted to sophisticated management work stations of the type described above. This opens up the possibility of reducing the amount of paper that is used, since the work station screen can be considered a desk-top, with all the 'paper-work' available in 'folders' or 'filing cabinets', or created on the screen. Letters and reports also need to be sent to other managers. Selecting the telephone icon, in our example, causes the work station to be linked to another computer via a modem, and thus enables information to be transmitted over a telephone line. Microcomputers may also be linked to each other by means of a local area network as described below.

Using a local area network

Figure 4.8 shows a number of microcomputers linked together by a cable to provide direct communication between the users of the microcomputers. Each user can access the disk units, printers and a modem link. The control of these devices is through microcomputers and special software.

Users can process work at their local microcomputer work stations, using software and data downloaded from the shared disk into the microcomputer's memory. Creation, deletion, and accessing data on the shared disk is handled by the file server which receives commands from the users. Only authorised users can change or delete information on any particular file, and reading the file can also be restricted.

The printer server receives requests for printing, and queues these up for the various printers. Some jobs in the queue may be

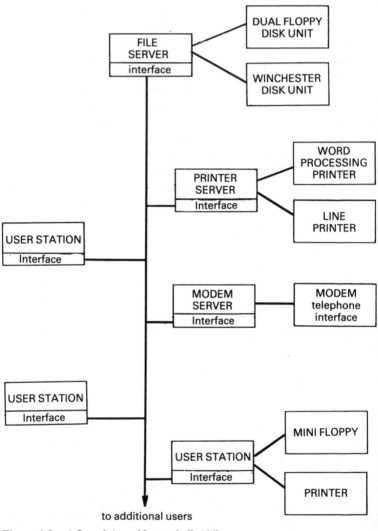

Figure 4.8 A Local Area Network (LAN)

dealt with before other jobs, according to the priorities allocated to them.

In a large company, users may need to access the company's

central computer or link to external computers, such as the Prestel viewdata system, through the modem server.

A local area network may be used for electronic mail, that is, the sending and receiving of messages and memoranda. Messages may be stored automatically if the recipient's microcomputer is not ready to receive a message. Confirmation of receipt of documents can be requested by the sender.

Each user on the system can have a personal diary in which notes can be entered. A *schedule grid* showing appointments and meetings for each week can be displayed on the screen and printed if required. A *reminder* file can be used to notify users about the activities they should carry out on a particular day.

A manager or secretary can arrange an appointment by selecting the appointments scheduling option and then entering the desired date, time and recipients (people who are invited to attend a meeting, for instance). The system will check the manager's diary and those of the recipients, to make sure everyone is available, and then will send messages to all the recipients.

Office automation software of this type will increasingly be used to reduce the time wasted on telephoning, and finding the person is not available, and the number of memoranda and letters that are sent through internal and external postal systems.

Teletex

Another form of electronic mail service is provided by the Teletex service, which allows communications between countries who have compatible services. Teletex enables desk-to-desk messages to be sent at speeds up to 3500 words per minute, compared to conventional Telex which has a maximum transmission rate of 80 words per minute.

National telecommunications administrations (PTTs), who are represented on the International Telegraph and Telephone Consultative Committee (CCITT), have discussed teletex standards and made technical recommendations for terminals. Various manufacturers provide sophisticated multi-function teletex terminals, which are microcomputers and can run word processing and business software.

The software offered with a teletex terminal may include basic and extended word-processing facilities, local teletex functions, automatic text assembly for letter generation, record processing (for example, sorting, merging and selective searching of information) and arithmetic functions. This means that teletex subscribers can prepare correspondence, orders, invoices, contracts, and so on, on these terminals, and send these to subscribers in other countries via communications networks.

5

Data Processing

Overview

The successful operation of many organisations depends on the use of up-to-date information held on their central computer. Files of data are held on employees, including their pay rate, tax code and other deductions, so that their pay can be worked out automatically by the computer. Payslips are produced but the salaries may be paid directly into the employees' bank accounts by transferring pay information to the banks electronically.

Most financial calculations will be carried out on the computer, including stock valuations which form part of an inventory or stock control system. Using software packages and microcomputers, it is possible for even small companies to set up an integrated accountancy system which links, for example, company sales, order entry and invoicing, and stock control (see Chapter 7).

Before such a system is purchased, an analysis of the company's present method of operation needs to be carried out, so that as precise a specification as possible can be drawn up. Once a system has been decided on, further preparation will include training staff in the new procedures, and setting up a suitable environment for the computer and data files. The system will be brought 'live' gradually by running parts of it in parallel with the existing clerical system. These stages are known as systems analysis, design and implementation. In a large organisation, they would be carried out by the data processing department, who would also be involved in designing and writing programs, or implementing software packages.

A time-consuming task is the conversion of manual files to computer files. This is a one-off task, but vitally important, as the files need to be accurate and complete. When the system is running, the files will be updated regularly with new information. All data entry needs to be controlled, so that mistakes in keying in information can be detected, and corrected as far as possible.

As systems are becoming more integrated, the computer files are no longer held separately for each application but are set up as a data base. Special software is available called Data Base Management Systems (DBMS) which enable technical staff to set up relationships between items of data. The aim is to allow easy but controlled access to this data by many different users, and at the same time ensure that the data is processed quickly and is kept secure.

The procedures necessary for successful commercial data processing are similar whether small or large computer systems are used. However, the scale and complexity of large computer systems require extensive data processing experience, whereas smaller systems can be run by business users who have only a basic knowledge of file processing on a microcomputer, so long as procedures are set up for controlling the running of the system and these are followed carefully.

A file processing and reporting example

This example illustrates some data processing principles and terminology. The system is based on a sequential file so that it can be used as a 'practice' example with a microcomputer that has a cassette or disk unit. A commercially usable system would be based on direct access disk files, which would be structured so that information could be accessed directly by means of indexes or other methods. Sequential files need to be read sequentially from the beginning until the required information has been located, which is much slower than direct access, but in the example the complete small file is loaded and held in the computer's memory.

The example is a stock recording program which enables you to set up a file containing stock records. Each stock record contains a number of fields, which are:

A stock number, i.e. a part or commodity number;
A description which can be a mixture of alphabetic and numeric characters;

The unit cost which is the cost of one unit of stock quantity – the monetary units must be consistent throughout the file;
The order quantity, i.e. the standard reorder quantity;
The reorder level any items whose stock is below this level will appear in the reorder list;
The stock quantity is the current stock level for this item;
The stock value which is calculated automatically whenever the unit cost or stock quantity is changed

The first stage is to set up the computer file by adding records to a new file. You are asked whether the file to be used is a new or existing file at the beginning of the computer run, whether it is a cassette or disk file, and what is its name. Next, a menu will appear on the screen as shown in Figure 5.1, and by selecting A you can add records to the file, by keying in the data in response to the questions that appear on the screen:

STOCK NUMBER ?
DESCRIPTION?

.
.
.

STOCK LEVEL?

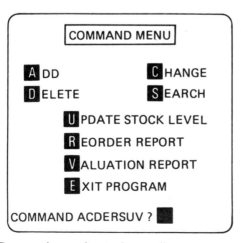

Figure 5.1 Command menu for stock recording program

After each record has been keyed in, you are asked:

ACCEPT DATA Y/N?

If your response is Y, then you have the option of continuing to add more records, or alternatively returning to the main menu. If your response is N, then the data is not stored, but you can key it in again, or return to the main menu to select another option.

After you have set up a file of data, you may want to obtain a valuation report (an example is shown in Figure 5.2).

At some stage, you may want to add further records for new stock items, delete records for stock items no longer held, and make changes to records. In the example, you can do this by selecting options A, D or C.

```
OUTPUT TO SCREEN OR PRINTER, S/P? S

            VALUATION REPORT
            ------------------

    STK NO   DESCRIPTION   STK QTY    VALUE
    ---------------------------------------------
      1234   PENS              15    675.00
      2340   PENCILS           50    600.00
      2679   ERASERS            8     40.00
      3456   RULERS            20    520.00
      4567   WRITING PADS      40   1400.00
      4568   NOTE BOOKS        60   2400.00
      6770   LABELS            70   1050.00
      6775   PINS              40    600.00
      6979   ENVELOPES         40    800.00
      7050   CASH BOOKS        30    660.00
    ---------------------------------------------
                            TOTAL   8745.00
    ---------------------------------------------


CONTINUE OR MENU?
```

Figure 5.2   A stock valuation report

You can make a change to any of the fields in the stock record except the stock number, since the latter is used to identify the record to be changed. Stock numbers can only be changed by deleting the record, and then adding the information as a new record.

When more stock comes in for existing items, or is sent out or used, the stock level is updated by selecting the U option from the main menu. This will cause a screen of information to appear as shown in Figure 5.3.

```
STOCK NUMBER TO UPDATE? 4567

RECORD NO 5

STOCK NUMBER          4567

DESCRIPTION           WRITING PADS

CURRENT STOCK 40

STOCK AJUSTMENT +/-?
```

Figure 5.3   The 'stock update' screen display

You then can enter a + or − number to adjust the stock, and a revised stock level will be shown. As for the previous data entry, you will be asked whether the data should be accepted or not, so that if you have made a mistake the adjustment will not be applied to the record.

Another option which is often required is a search, S in this case, to find records which have certain descriptions. For example, if the stock was concerned with stationery items, the stock quantities of notebooks, cash books, and so on, could be listed by keying in BOOKS as the search word.

Note that all the reports in the example can be displayed on the screen or listed on a printer, depending on the reply to the question:

OUTPUT TO SCREEN OR PRINTER, S/P?

which appears on the screen as part of the output routine.

An example of a reorder report is shown in Figure 5.4. This is

```
     OUTPUT  TO  SCREEN  OR  PRINTER,  S/P?  S

                REORDER  REPORT
                ---------------

     STK  NO    DESCRIPTION    ORD  QTY    COST
     -------------------------------------------
          1234  PENS                60  2700.00
          2679  ERASERS             50   250.00
          3456  RULERS             100  2600.00
          4567  WRITING  PADS      200  7000.00
          6979  ENVELOPES          200  4000.00
          7050  CASH  BOOKS        100  2200.00
     -------------------------------------------
                              TOTAL    18750.00
     -------------------------------------------

     CONTINUE  OR  MENU?
```

Figure 5.4   A reorder report

produced automatically when the option R is chosen from the main menu.

When all the changes to the file have been made, and the required reports output, the option E is chosen from the main menu. The exit routine then displays:

SAVE CURRENT FILE, Y/N?

This allows you to save the current file on cassette tape or disk or abandon it. You can overwrite an existing file with the new version by giving it the same name or create a new file with a different name. Finally, the computer will display a message confirming that a file has been saved.

The program for this example is given in *Computer Programming with the Commodore 64* (see page 46). You could develop the example further by incorporating more data entry checks, as described in the next section, and include more options such as a sort, complete stock listing, and different types of reports, for example, a stock listing in decreasing value of stock.

Data entry checks

It is very easy to make mistakes when keying in data. In commercial systems, it is usual to have the data entered checked by another operator keying the information in again during a verification stage. If the two sets of data do not match exactly, then either the first or the second operator has made a mistake, and this can be corrected.

In addition to this type of verification, it is common for the data to be validated by a program which has been set up to check certain important data items. For example, if an account number is numeric, it can be checked to make sure that all the characters keyed into that field were numeric. Also, a check digit can be added to the number which is directly related to the digits contained in the number. You will find an example of a check digit on the back cover of this book as part of the ISBN (International Standard Bibliography Number). You may like to check this number using the steps in the following example.

The ISBN of *The Pocket Calculator* (Teach Yourself Books), by the present authors is 0-340-33836-9. The last digit (9) is the check digit and the arithmetic process applied to the number, comprising the preceding digits, should result therefore in an answer of 9. Starting with the final digit (6), each digit is successively multiplied by 2, 3, 4, 5, etc., as shown in Figure 5.5. These 'weighted' multiples are then totalled, in this case to 145. The total is then divided by 11 and the *remainder* noted (in this case 2), finally this remainder is subtracted from 11 to give the check digit.

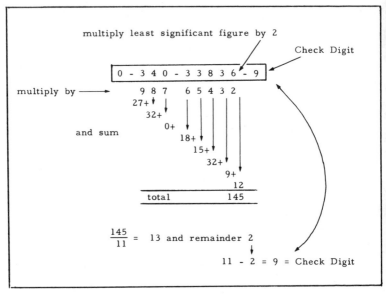

Figure 5.5   Check digit calculation

Because of the use made of 11, this method is known as the modulus-11 check digit system. If the number is entered incorrectly (e.g. 0-340-33863-9), then the above calculation will not agree that the check digit is 9 and the ISBN would be rejected by the computer.

Another type of check is required if a number can be within a range. For example, date entries could have range checks specified for the day (01 to 31) and the month (01 to 12).

Commercial systems development

The development of a large commercial system can involve many years of work for an experienced team of systems analysts, programmers and potential users. This time is reduced substantially for small business systems when commercially-available software packages are used with microcomputers.

This section looks at the tasks that need to be carried out for a large system. However, many of these tasks should be included when developing a microcomputer-based system, since the cost to a company, if a system fails and important data is lost, can be very high.

Systems analysis
The first stage is called systems analysis. This is concerned with carrying out an initial exploratory study called a *feasibility study*. Once a decision has been made to develop and implement the system, a more detailed investigation needs to be carried out to determine the system requirements.

At the end of the systems analysis stage, it should be possible to specify the requirements to be met by the systems design stage. It is also necessary, for proper control, to estimate the cost and time schedules to be met by the project group as the application proceeds.

Systems design
The systems design stage is concerned with specifying the precise relationship between the input system, output system and files. This needs to be decided before any individual programs can be written. These relationships will be illustrated by charts. Detailed specifications of all the individual subsystems will include exact formats of the input, output, and any information to be held in files. Some flexibility should be built in, if possible, otherwise subsequent changes could mean programs have to be amended.

The importance of testing cannot be overemphasised. Programs may be written and tested independently, and at a later stage tested together, to ensure that the total system is working correctly. Adequate time needs to be allowed for program and system testing, using data supplied by the systems analysis team, and also for producing documentation.

Good documentation will make subsequent amendments to programs easier. In addition, comprehensive and comprehensible documentation needs to be produced for the users of the system;

less documentation is necessary for systems which are menu driven, and hence easy to use.

System implementation

A number of important tasks need to be planned and carried out as part of the system implementation. One major task is the conversion of the existing files. The problem facing management here is that this is a one-off task, and while it is being carried out the existing system must be kept running. Possible solutions include using temporary staff or a bureau, overtime working, or trying to fit the task into a slack period.

The file conversion task needs careful supervision as it may be found that the data is not complete. Any gaps in the data will have to be filled in when producing the computer files.

At an early stage, during program writing and file conversion, orders may need to be placed for new office equipment to accommodate the computer, and training and retraining of staff needs to be started. This will help to ensure successful running of the system when it becomes 'live'.

The system may be installed in stages while the current system is still being operated. This parallel running of the old and new system will cease once the complete system has been installed and is working as specified. It is important to ensure that the installed system is performing according to the specification. This testing should involve the users, before the system is finally handed over by the project team, and is called *user acceptance testing*.

After some time, the system may grow in size. Continuous monitoring will pick up problems such as degradation of performance due to increased data volumes and user activity.

Data bases

Companies may keep many different computer files of business information on disks. Magnetic tape may be used for storage of 'historical' data which is not currently in use and may only be referred to occasionally.

It is often advantageous to set up a corporate data base on disk which holds all the items of information used by the organisation's different computer programs. This avoids the problem of duplicated information kept on separate files being out of step because the files were updated at different times. When a data base is used, all the different application programs can use the same up-to-date information.

Another advantage is that the information held on the data base can be controlled more easily than if independent files were used. One person, the Data Base Administrator (DBA), or a team of people, can be put in charge of the company's data. One of their tasks is to ensure that the data base is kept up-to-date and secure, by setting up security procedures as discussed later in Chapter 10.

Company data bases can be very large and take up a large amount of disk storage. The data base is set up and maintained using a software package called a Data Base Management System (DBMS). Different data items can be linked in a specified way to give a particular structure according to the type of DBMS used. The software also provides facilities to give users easy access to the data, provided that they have the required authorisation.

Users need not be aware of how the data is stored physically on the disk. The DBA creates and maintains the data base, making sure that the data is stored efficiently. The data base is reorganised when necessary to maintain high performance. This means the DBA has to have technical knowledge of how the data base is constructed and used.

Some microcomputer data base software has been written especially for business users, and can provide a useful means of handling data files. However, there is still the problem of controlling the use of the data and making sure that it is accurate.

6

Word Processing

Overview

A word processor is a computer which has software for editing, reformatting and printing text. Text is usually entered from a keyboard and may be stored on disk for subsequent retrieval. Most of the systems allow editing to be carried out on a visual display unit which displays a 'page' of text. Reformatting facilities enable the alteration of margins, positioning of headings, justification of the right-hand margin, etc.

The systems may be stand-alone (self-contained), but are capable of being linked to other word processors and central computer systems. *Shared-logic* and *shared-facility* refer to systems which either have a number of VDU's linked to one processor, or share disk storage and printers; these systems may also be called *shared-resource* systems.

Systems may be dedicated to word processing, although some arithmetic and data processing functions are often included. Word processing software is also available on general-purpose large computers and microcomputers, allowing it to be interfaced to other programs for applications involving text editing or printed letters and reports.

Dedicated systems usually have sophisticated software with many facilities, and keyboards with special function keys. However, even low-cost WP packages on microcomputers may have useful functions and their use is widespread in offices.

Dedicated shared-logic systems are found in large companies where they are used by skilled word processing operators as a replacement for the typing pool, and bureaux specialising in word processing have also been established. In these environments, it is essential to have a WP supervisor who manages the operation, since the storage and retrieval of letters and reports need to be carefully controlled. Different shared printers and stationery may be used, and confidentiality of information, in reports and letters, can be an important issue.

Common features

Most word processing systems have a number of features that are considered to be essential. Sophisticated word processing software usually has a very large range of facilities, some of which are discussed later.

The original text may be typed, handwritten, on tape, or in shorthand. This is entered from the keyboard at speed, particularly if the system has a *word wraparound* facility that automatically transfers text to the next line when the right-hand margin is reached. In most systems, the text will be displayed on an 80-column screen as it is entered.

The settings of the margins and tabs are shown on a *ruler line* and these can be changed by the operator to suit the particular application. One or more *status lines* may also be displayed, showing the cursor position as a line and column number, the page number and the file reference. The cursor is usually a flashing line or square.

The operator may carry out some editing of the text as it is being entered. For example, if a mistake is made when keying in a word, the cursor can be moved to it, and the correction made. Words, sentences and paragraphs can be deleted, inserted, changed and moved. At any time, the text can be saved on disk for subsequent retrieval. A long report may be saved in sections, and each section edited separately.

After editing, the text can be printed out. Daisy-wheel or ink-jet printers are usually used for 'letter-quality' printing, although high-quality matrix printers may also be used. It is useful to have a variety of print enhancements available, such as underline, double strike and bold. Proportional spacing is available with some printers; this spaces the letters according to their size to give a good appearance to the text. Examples of some printing styles for a dot matrix printer are shown in Figure 6.1. The versatility of this type of printer means that it is important to ensure that the chosen word

```
     This is the normal printing obtained when the
printer is first switched on.  By including commands
to the printer with the text in a word processing
package it is possible to exercise control over the
printer. The features available on the printer will
vary according to the make and model.
```

The printing can be 'emphasised' as in this
paragraph. The printer is switched into this mode by
including designated code numbers in the word
processing text. The word processor recognises that
these codes should not be printed but sent instead
unchanged, direct to the printer.

The printer has its own memory which stores these
instructions, using the appropriate font until further
instructions are received.

It can be very useful to have a condensed mode
for direct quotes, footnotes etc.

```
     Another mode that is very useful, particularly
for headings, is the Enlarged Mode, i.e.
```

The Enlarged Mode

```
     Another feature of the printer is that it has an
'underline' mode.  This is very useful because
with traditional printers underlining is printed on
the next line and is therefore difficult to
incorporate within text.
```

Figure 6.1   Some dot matrix printing styles

processing package has the ability to send correct control codes to
the printer.

Most text needs to be reformatted at some stage. The right-hand
margin may be *justified* (so that words are lined up at the margin as
in a book) by setting the justification function to ON. Justification
may be set to OFF for letters, which gives a ragged right-hand edge,
so that it appears as though the letters have been typed individually
on an electric typewriter. When text is justified, the spacing in
between the words is adjusted to be as even as possible.

Further requirements for reports are page formatting and pagination control. Page formatting includes setting top and bottom
margins, and inserting headings and footings. In addition, a facility
may be provided for putting page numbers in different positions,

centrally or alternately left and right. To avoid odd lines appearing at the bottom of a page, referred to as *widow lines*, page breaks may be set in places where the page should end. This facility is known as pagination control.

It is convenient to have margin settings, and other control settings, set to commonly used values, for example, a page length of seventy-two lines, when the system is started up. The operator then only needs to change these 'standard' settings when required.

Standard letters and documents

A common requirement is to use the same text in a letter or document but to *personalise* it with details which relate, for example, to a particular customer.

Figure 6.2 shows a standard letter with the positions where variable information is to be inserted indicated by *variable names*, such as title or surname, marked at each end by ampersands (&). The variable information is held on a disk file (*df*) called *ehdemds.dta*, with each person's details being held in one record. The variable items in each record are listed in the *rv* (record variables) command. When the letter is merged with the data file, using the mail-merge option, each letter will be addressed individually when printed.

The /O in some of the address lines on the standard letter indicates that if the data field referenced for the current record is empty, then a blank line will not be left in the address. For example, if the person's position and the county are unknown, then the address will consist of only six lines with no blank lines. The *sv* (set variable) command allows a variable to be set to some value which can be altered from run to run – in this case, the date to be shown on each letter is set at the beginning of the run.

The word processing software used for this example is MicroPro International's WordStar package, which is available for many microcomputers. Other systems have similar facilities which are implemented in a different way.

Another use of the mail-merge facility is for legal documents which must be completely accurate. Documents may be standard or made up from existing paragraphs held on disk with the addition of

```
.pl 72
.mt 10
.op
.sv date, 10th November 1982
.df a:ehdemds.dta
.rv surname,initials,title,position,company,address1,address2,town,county,pc
```

```
        &title& &initials&  &surname&
        &position/O&
        &company/O&
        &address1&
        &address2/O&
        &town&
        &county/O&                              &date&
        &pc&


        Dear &title& &surname&

        Thank you for your enquiry regarding our seminar on Electronic
        Office Applications.  The programme for the seminar is:

        9.30    Overview of the Electronic Office

        10.30   Coffee

        10.45   Practical sessions and demonstrations

        12.45   Lunch

        13.45   Analysis of system requirements

        15.15   Tea

        15.30   Problem areas - discussion

        The fee for the seminar is 75 pounds, including documentation,
        buffet lunch, morning and afternoon refreshments.  Please return
        your completed application form as soon as possible so that we
        can reserve a place for you.  We would be pleased to send you
        information on our other Electronic Office courses.

        Yours sincerely,

.pa
```

Figure 6.2   A 'standard' letter

some new paragraphs. Information pertaining to a particular client can then be added in the way described above.

Reports

Many changes are usually made between the original draft of a report and the final document. As well as sentences and paragraphs being altered, whole sections may be moved from one place to another, for example, an appendix may be created by moving material out of the main text. The whole appearance of the document may be changed with respect to headings, underlining and style of printing required. Tables in the report may have columns transferred or transposed. It is useful to have a facility for setting decimal tabs, so that the decimal points of numbers in columns can be aligned.

Some systems have special facilities for creating charts and graphs, and various shapes for these may be stored on disk and called up when required. Mathematical formulae may require the use of subscripts, superscripts and mathematical symbols. Some word processing systems have been designed especially for this type of work and allow equations to be created and edited on the screen. Formulae may be saved and merged into the text. The final report may be printed on a dual head daisy-wheel printer, so information can be directed to either wheel, one of which prints ordinary letters, and the other the mathematical symbols.

Some business reports may need the results of calculations to be incorporated. This may be done by interfacing the WP software to data processing programs, or these facilities may be available as part of the word processing system. For example, simple calculations may be performed such as vertical and horizontal addition of numbers in a table (including monetary amounts, transfer of totals and calculation of percentages).

Additional features

There are many more facilities that may be provided by a sophisticated word processing system. These tend to concentrate on making the system easier to use, and improving the appearance and accuracy of documents.

The appearance of documents can be improved by setting hyphens using a *hyphenation* facility. When the document is reformatted and a hyphenated word needs to be split over two lines, the hyphen will be shown, otherwise the word will appear without the hyphen. Without this facility, the whole of the long word has to be transferred to the next line if part of it has reached the right-hand margin. This may mean large spacing having to be left between words on the line to allow for the gap left by the long word.

Automatic *spelling verification* may be useful for some applications, particularly when complex technical terms are used. Standard dictionaries (of about 50000 words) and personal dictionaries (up to 5000 words) are provided by some systems. Documents can be checked for spelling against these dictionaries and any discrepancies highlighted on the screen for the operator to correct. In some cases, the word will be correct but not included in the dictionary; then the word can be added to the dictionary, so that over a period of time the initial general purpose dictionary becomes tailored to the specialist user, for example, an accountant or lawyer.

Sometimes one word may have been misspelt throughout the document. A *global search* and *replacement* facility allows each occurrence of the word to be found and replaced automatically with the correct word. Different options may be attached to this command. For example, every time the search word is found, the system may stop to allow the operator to change the word or not, or with another option the changes are made throughout the document without stopping. The distinction between upper and lower case may be disregarded by choosing a particular option, and the search may be forwards or backwards.

Most systems allow the text to be moved (scrolled) up or down the screen so that the operator can work on the required part of the document. If the document is wider than the screen, the exact appearance of the formatted document may not be available until it is printed, since long lines may be continued on the next line on the screen. Sideways scrolling allows continuation of text on the same line but only part of it will be viewed as it is scrolled to the left or right.

An alternative option that may be provided is to change the screen format to display more, but smaller, letters on each line. For example, with a home computer, the number of characters displayed on a line may be changed from 40 to 80, but the 80-column display may not be seen clearly on a television set and may require a monitor with a higher resolution. Most commercial systems use 80-column VDUs, and some of these can be changed to display 132 columns for wide documents.

In a professional word processing environment, the same type of work may be repeated over and over again. For these systems, it is useful to be able to program the steps required for a particular task. The program may consist of coded commands or English words corresponding to the function keys that the operator would normally press when carrying out the WP task.

This program can be called up when required by pressing a particular key. The program may be written down and keyed in originally or the function keys pressed by the operator may be 'remembered' by the system. This type of facility can save a considerable amount of time in word processing installations where some WP tasks are carried out on a regular basis.

Using WP with other software

Apart from the conventional uses of word processing systems, there are many applications where WP software can be interfaced to other programs to provide editing, formatting and printing facilities.

This section describes two quite different applications; one is based on large computers with sophisticated software for formatting text for publications, while the second application is run on a microcomputer and uses BASIC programs and a low-cost WP package.

A text processing application

Computers with advanced software are used by a company specialising in the production of various publications from information held on magnetic data files. The method used enables catalogues, telephone directories, tourists guides, dictionaries and electoral registers to be updated easily and quickly when required. The information is formatted in various ways to suit the requirements of the phototypesetting equipment to be used.

Customers can submit magnetic tapes or floppy disk files which contain information coded in different ways. These files are converted by specially-designed software into the format required by editing and text formatting programs. The software interprets the requirements for headings, margins, typefaces, small capitals, accents, foreign language, mathematical symbols and so on, and these are stored as *'record types'* next to the records of text.

Each record type number indicates a formatting requirement, and a table giving the meaning of the record types is used with the software. The meaning of the record types in the table can be changed. For example, information could be assigned a record type meaning *bold*; at a later stage, the printing could be in *italic* just by changing the meaning of the record type in the table.

The software interfaces with a word processing system which provides facilities for editing, justifying, printing, maintaining headings, setting margins, making indentations, and so on.

The software also produces magnetic tapes for driving different phototypesetters. A page at a time is built up in the computer's memory and output to the drive tape. The phototypesetting equipment uses this magnetic tape to produce each page on a roll of film. Space can be left for illustrations or advertisements which can be slotted in manually at a later stage.

Magnetic tapes are also produced for directly updating a large data base in the USA holding millions of characters of text. This forms the basis of an on-line information retrieval system which can be accessed by subscribers in the UK using terminals linked to the USA computer via a communications satellite.

A system for estate agents

This application is implemented on a microcomputer and uses word processing software in conjunction with specially-written BASIC programs. The main requirement of the system is to produce property details.

When a customer requests details of property in a certain price range, a selection can be made according to the type of property – private, residential, commercial/industrial, commercial/agricultural. The property is classified further by the type of structure – residential housing, flat, bungalow, maisonette, shop or factory – and whether it is freehold or leasehold. The details are displayed on the screen and only those of interest are printed.

A word processing package is used to produce 'follow-up' letters, which can be personalised using information such as names, addresses, properties of interest, date of enquiries, and so on, held on a disk file for each client.

7

Commercial Systems

Overview

Computers are used in business and commerce for a wide variety of applications. Many systems are based on large (mainframe) computers which have fast processors, huge memory and disk storage capacities. The financial applications of large industrial companies are processed on these types of systems, as are the transactions carried out by banks, insurance companies and building societies.

The banking system has to process millions of cheques daily, so that a method for automatically reading cheques is essential. Similarly, public utilities, such as electricity and gas boards, need to produce bills and process accounts rapidly for their many customers. More convenient methods for obtaining cash from one's bank account (by the use of cash cards) and for paying bills (through viewdata systems) have been developed. The trend is to reduce the amount of paper being used and to eliminate postal charges where possible.

The retailing industry, with its huge turnover of many different items of goods, has used new technology to improve profitability and the service to its customers. Point of sale terminals are widely used in large stores, resulting in the capture of information that allows management to respond quickly to current situations. Other devices, such as hand-held data entry terminals and adapted television sets, enable representatives to enter orders quickly into their companies' computers over the public telephone system, and to send and receive messages using viewdata systems.

Managers are able to plan more effectively through the use of software packages which allow alternatives to be tested, and also use computers to monitor the progress of the implemented plans.

Small companies can use microcomputers to process all their financial applications and can link various software modules to form an integrated business system, incorporating word processing and financial modelling for correspondence, reports and planning.

Banking

Banking was one of the first commercial systems to use computerised input forms in dealing with customers, namely, the MICR characters preprinted on to cheques. By preprinting the cheque serial number, the bank branch sorting code and the customer's account number, only the cheque amount remains to be added.

MICR is particularly suitable for cheques because of the large amount of handling involved. All cheque transactions have to pass through *clearing banks* where they are sorted by branch codes allowing the cheques to be related to individual account numbers. To curtail some of the cheque handling involved, banks discourage customers from asking for their cheques to be returned with their bank statements. However, auditors and tax inspectors may require the production of the original cheque as evidence of payment, and so the practice cannot be entirely discontinued.

The advantage of using MICR, compared to OCR in this environment, is that MICR characters are not affected by marks made across them, whereas folds or marks can cause OCR documents to be misread.

Many cheques are paid in to a bank together with a preprinted payment slip, for example, an electricity bill. The bill has account and payment details printed twice on it by a computer. The customer keeps one part of the bill for reference, and the 'tear-off' slip is returned to the electricity board's computer centre after payment, so that the customer's account can be updated. Hence, this type of bill is known as a *turn-around* document.

Bills contain more variable information than a cheque, such as the customer's account number, name and address, the last and previous meter readings, electricity units consumed, price per unit and total amount to be paid, in the case of an electricity bill. This information needs to be produced rapidly on line printers for millions of customers, making OCR the usual choice rather than

MICR. The production of MICR documents requires special magnetic ink and greater accuracy, and is more costly.

In addition to processing individual cheques, the banks also have to process standing orders and direct debits for customers and to credit the customers' accounts with credit transfers, for example, when dealing with the payment of wages.

Banks may provide customers with cash cards to enable them to obtain cash from machines called cash dispensers situated inside and outside of branches of the bank. The cash card has a magnetic stripe which contains details of the customer's account number and an identity number; these are invisible to the human eye. When the card is put into the cash dispenser machine, the customer has to key in the identity number corresponding to the one held in the magnetic stripe on the card. If the amount requested does not exceed the limit allowed and there is sufficient money in the account, the cash is dispensed in notes to the customer, and the balance in the account is debited automatically. Customers may also ask to see their bank balances which are printed out by some machines.

Further developments of the cash card include a credit card which has a fixed value. When it is used in a transaction, the information held in the microchip memory within the card is updated to reduce the amount remaining.

The advantages to be obtained from reducing the amount of cheque handling is leading banks to consider ways of directly debiting accounts by the use of on-line systems. This approach to banking is given the name *Electronic Funds Transfer* (EFT). The most widespread use of EFT is likely to be in retailing, where by presenting a bank card, the customers will have their accounts debited immediately through an on-line system linking the store's point of sales terminal to the bank's computer. Banks are also likely to offer these services through the so-called 'homebanking' view-data systems.

Homebanking

Homebanking is now a reality for customers holding an account with certain banks and a building society. The 24 hour service is provided through Prestel, as described in Chapter 4. As well as giving access to all the Prestel services (news, weather, entertainment, and so on), customers have a wide range of banking, buying and selling opportunities.

You can look at your account on your TV screen, and transfer funds between your bank and building society. Correspondence between you and the bank can be via the screen, avoiding postal charges. Also domestic bills can be paid through the system at any time.

Many companies advertise on Prestel, so you can shop from home by placing orders (obtaining discounts in some cases), or select holidays and make reservations. You may wish to place an advertisement, for instance when selling domestic equipment which is no longer required, and these advertisements may be free, similar to the service offered by some local papers. There is the possibility of linking to other networks through Prestel, such as those providing telesoftware (see p. 62).

Obviously, as financial matters are a major service, the organisations providing this type of facility need to be particularly careful to ensure that no one can gain unauthorised access to your accounts. One organisation has as many as ten security checks, some of which are not revealed even to customers.

Retailing

Retailers initially used computers for accountancy applications, like any other business. A major advantage in having the accounts computerised is the closer control obtainable over creditors. Large scale purchasing can also lead to substantial discounts, providing payments are made on time. A computerised system helps to ensure that these deadlines are met and not overlooked.

A retailing business is dependent on effective stock management, and therefore, as experience with computer systems grew, more attention was paid to monitoring the stock holding on a computer. Conventional accountancy systems allow the organisation to monitor the stock which has been brought into the company. Retailing, however, has special needs, in that stock goes out (i.e. is sold) in small quantities, and unlike the manufacturing industry the stock movement is not preplanned. There is therefore a special need to monitor details of the items sold, as accurately and as quickly as possible.

The development of cash tills has been with a view to the automatic recording of items sold. Initially, the conventional tally rolls in cash tills were replaced by ones which had transactions printed on them in OCR characters. This allowed the retained tally roll to be processed as input to a computer system at the end of the day or week.

In some instances, particularly in dress shops, individual items had a tag attached to them that had holes representing the stock number punched into it. The tag was removed at the sales desk. At the end of the day or week, all the punched tags were sent away to be processed by a computer system, thereby updating the stock files.

Point of sale terminals

As technology developed, alternative means of marking stock items became available; the most common being magnetic stripe tags and bar coding. To gain advantage from these, it is necessary to be able to capture the stock details at the time of the sale. The cash till therefore becomes a data entry device, whereby the information on the magnetic stripe ticket or a bar code can be read automatically by a *wand*. The information read from the wand may be combined with any other details keyed in by the cashier and stored on a cassette tape or disk, or the information may be passed directly into a central computer system through a point of sale (POS) terminal.

The use of a POS not only ensures that the computerised stock records are correctly maintained, but also speeds up significantly the feedback of information to management. Sales in a retail store are influenced by displays, special offers and regional differences in taste. On-line point of sales systems allow management to respond to what is happening now, as opposed to only being able to review the situation in retrospect. In large department stores, takings might be monitored hourly and action taken immediately to respond to problems of low takings and goods being out-of-stock.

An on-line system also allows management to monitor the general level of activity at specific POS terminals and to deploy sales staff more effectively. Some of the POS terminals can also read credit cards and hence help to reduce bad debts, for example, where the credit limit is being exceeded. In this case, the POS terminal will alert the finance office to send a manager, while a code on the POS terminal indicates to the sales assistant that the customer is to be detained until the problem is resolved.

In order to use POS terminals, stock items must be coded. In the case of large retailing groups, the codes used may be those developed by the company. There are further benefits to be obtained, however, if the codes follow an agreed standard within the industry. An example of industry-wide standard coding is the use of bar coding within the food industry. This not only allows items premarked by the supplier to be read at any POS terminal accepting the bar codes, but also allows the supplier and vendor to exchange trading information with the minimum need for recoding to suit a particular computer system. As previously mentioned, the POS terminal will eventually also have an electronic funds transfer capability to complete the sales side of the transaction.

Hand-held terminals

Another area where the retailing industry has gained by the use of computer technology is in the use of hand-held terminals by suppliers' representatives. During the day, the representative keys details of the firm orders into a hand-held data entry unit. At the end of the day, the unit is connected to a telephone in the representative's home or hotel (see Figure 1.12), and all the orders are transferred down the phone line to the supplier's computer. Sales representatives get involved in a great deal of paperwork which has to be sent to head office. Using a portable data entry unit reduces the paperwork and also reduces the order processing time, to the advantage of the purchasers.

Alternatively, information can be exchanged between representatives and their companies' offices by using a viewdata system and suitably-adapted television sets. This two-way communication has the advantage that representatives can find out the stock situation of various items and can receive messages through the viewdata's 'mailbox' facility. A company may have its own private viewdata system linked to its data processing system, or it may use a bureau which specialises in this type of service.

Business planning

Planning is at the heart of most commercial organisations. By its nature, planning requires that the company's general policies and strategy are followed through down to the minutest detail. The best decisions come from examining several alternatives. In practice, because of the detail involved, planning can be a time-consuming activity, and so there is often not the time to develop and examine alternative plans.

Management's problems are not over when the plans have been developed. Due to changing circumstances the plans may need to be revised, and once implemented, the data will need to be updated in line with progress.

Using computers considerably aids planning and removes many of the above difficulties. It becomes possible for managers to ask and pursue many more 'what if . . .' options, as the computer can rapidly recalculate the effects. The use of computers also speeds up and simplifies the updating of plans in line with actual progress achieved.

Two examples are discussed below. The first illustrates the use of an electronic spreadsheet software package, ideal for 'what if . . .' questions. The second example illustrates bar charts that are obtainable from Critical Path Planning packages.

Electronic spreadsheets
Electronic spreadsheet packages allow the user to build up a worksheet on a computer screen. The particular advantage of these packages is that, once built up, any numeric changes made to the worksheet immediately cause the computer to recalculate any dependent values. As the spreadsheet can be built up by the user and printouts obtained without any programming knowledge, these packages are powerful tools for 'what if . . .' investigations.

The spreadsheet is initially presented to the user as a blank 'sheet' consisting of many rows and columns, for example, 200 rows by 50 columns. The computer screen provides a 'window' on the work-sheet, and the user can move the window to view any part of the worksheet.

There are three types of entry that the user can make on the worksheet after positioning the screen cursor over the required part of the worksheet. An item of text, heading, label, and so on, can be entered simply by typing it in. Similarly, numeric values can be typed in directly from a keyboard. The third type of entry is a formula. A formula is entered by specifying the appropriate coordinates (row and column identifiers) of the required *cells* on the worksheet, having previously positioned the cursor over the cell where the formula is to be implemented. For example:

$$+ A6 + D7$$

may be entered when the cursor was over E8. The *result* of adding the value currently in A6 (column A, row 6) to that in D7, will then be displayed in E8. Subsequently, changing the value in A6 and/or D7 will cause the result in E8 to be recalculated immediately and displayed in E8.

An example of a worksheet designed to show the profitability or otherwise of a product is given in Figure 7.1. Figure 7.2 shows the formulae used in the worksheet. The column notation A, B, C, and so on, and the row numbers are not usually printed out around the edge of the worksheet, but have been in this instance, to aid the discussion and to clarify the formulae appearing in Figure 7.2.

Production information is entered into column B, rows 8, 9, 13 and 14. From this information, the computer calculates the material cost per unit and displays the result in B18. The formula used is B8*B13 (see Figure 7.2). Note that * is used to signify multiplication. Unit labour costs are calculated in a similar manner and displayed in B19. The total direct cost (i.e. materials and labour) is displayed in B21.

The sales information is entered in F8 and unit price in F10. From this, the expected income can be calculated as F8*F10 and this result is displayed in F16.

A simple profit or loss summary is then built up in the lower part of the worksheet. The income calculated and displayed in F16 is carried over to E30. The unit direct cost (B21) is multiplied by the total demand (F8) and the result displayed in D31. Overheads entered in to D32 are added to the direct costs to give total costs in D34. The total costs in D34 is transferred to E34. Finally, the profit or loss resulting from subtracting the total costs in E34 from the income in E30 is calculated and displayed in E36.

Making any changes in the basic data, for example, altering the unit price in F10, will instantly cause all dependent values to be recalculated throughout the worksheet resulting in a revised profit or loss value.

```
            PRODUCT: ZAP Cleaner              DATE: 12.3.83
            ====================              =============

            PRODUCTION INFO               SALES INFORMATION
            ---------------               -----------------
COSTS
-----
Material        6.23 /litre      Demand          2000  Cans
Labour          4.75 /hour
                                 Unit Price       7.50

WORK CONTENT
------------
Material         .5 litres
Labour           .22 hours

UNIT COST                        INCOME       15000.00
---------                        ------
Material        3.12
Labour          1.05
                -----
Direct          4.16
                -----



        ----------------------------------------

                PROFIT/LOSS SUMMARY
                -------------------

        Income                        15000.00
            less Direct      8320.00
                 Overheads    3000.00
                             ----------
                             13320.00 13320.00
                                      ----------
                        PROFIT/LOSS    1680.00
                                      ==========
```

Figure 7.1 A spreadsheet to calculate profit

Critical Path Planning

In addition to using the computer to carry out financial analyses, the computer can be used in the subsequent planning of any decisions implemented. Figure 7.3 shows a simplified plan, for the launch of a product, as a network. Each activity, such as print packaging, is shown as a box. The network diagram shows that this activity can only *follow* the design packaging activity and *must precede* the package first batch activity. It also shows that, for reference purposes, this activity has been assigned the number 40 and it will take three weeks.

```
              A          B          C          D          E          F

 1                   PRODUCT: ZAP Cleaner            DATE: 12.3.83
 2                   ====================            =============
 3
 4                 PRODUCTION INFO                 SALES INFORMATION
 5                 ---------------                 -----------------
 6       COSTS
 7       -----
 8       Material        6.23 /litre        Demand              2000
 9       Labour          4.75 /hour
10                                          Unit Price          7.50
11       WORK CONTENT
12       ------------
13       Material         .5 litres
14       Labour           .22 hours
15
16       UNIT COST                          INCOME       +F8*F10
17       ---------                          ------
18       Material    +B8*B13
19       Labour      +B9*B14
20                   ---------
21       Direct      +B18+B19
22                   ---------
23
24
25                   ---------------------------------------
26
27                        PROFIT/LOSS SUMMARY
28                        -------------------
29
30              Income                              +F16
31                 less Direct        +B21*F8
32                      Overheads     5000.00
33                                    -------------------
34                                    +D31+D32       +D34
35                                                   ---------
36                      PROFIT/LOSS    +E30-E34
37                                     =========
```

Figure 7.2   The spreadsheet showing the formulae used

The information contained in Figure 7.3 is the data required by a Critical Path Planning (CPP) package. From an analysis of this data, the computer produces a schedule as shown in Figure 7.4. A bar of *C*s indicates that the activity must be carried over the indicated time period. A bar of *S*s indicates the time period scheduled for other activities, and the hyphens indicate the extent that these schedules can slip without extending the total duration period (eight weeks, in this case).

In practice, with a project consisting of perhaps 500 activities, it becomes very laborious to develop a schedule without a computer.

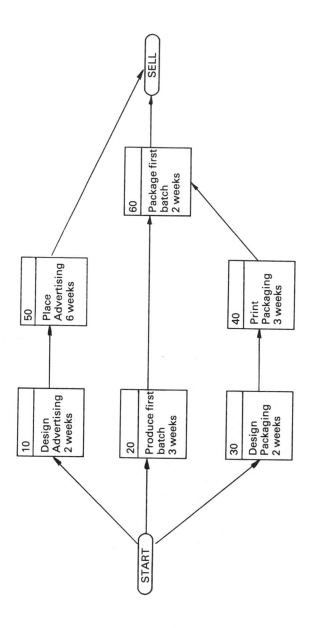

Figure 7.3 Network plan for launch of a product

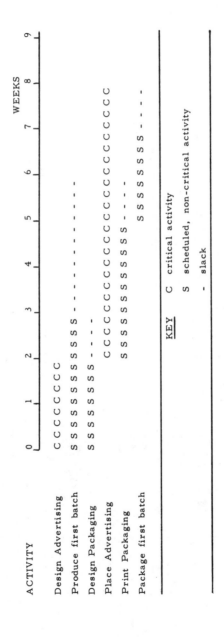

Figure 7.4 A critical path schedule

It is equally important to be able to calculate the effects of delays, and to reschedule as the project progresses. Thus a computer is of use throughout the duration of the project.

Integrated business systems

Various integrated business systems have been implemented on microcomputers. These systems are suitable for small companies, for example, manufacturers and distributors of goods, or firms of accountants and management consultants.

The requirements of each organisation will vary, but the software is written in a flexible way to allow a variety of systems to be put together. This flexibility is provided by the modular structure of the integrated business system, with each module comprising programs for processing a particular function, as shown in Figure 7.5.

In some cases, further modules can be added, either written by programmers within the company, or as a special order from the software supplier. The latter option can be very expensive, and

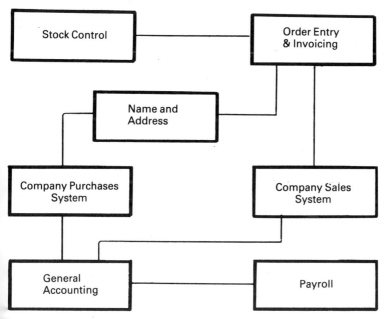

Figure 7.5   A modular integrated business system

usually is not viable unless a group of users with similar requirements share the cost.

Files may be held on floppy or hard disks depending on the size of company and factors such as the number of employees or items of stock. For example, if a company has several thousand items of stock, the stock file will generally be held on a hard disk.

The individual modules may be purchased separately and a system built up gradually to make the implementation of all the necessary office procedures easier. Further modules may be added as the company's business grows, or when requirements change.

The payroll software will require updating when legislation changes. This service may be included in a software maintenance charge, so that, for example, the user does not need to consult tax tables when a change occurs, but will be provided with a new program disk incorporating all the changes.

The advantage of having an integrated system, such as the one shown in Figure 7.5, is illustrated by the following example, which considers the effect of generating invoices for various stock items.

When an invoice is created, stock levels are adjusted automatically, and used to produce an analysis of stock movement, which allows the company to see which goods are selling best. The names and addresses of the customers being invoiced are accessed automatically from a central file.

Invoice details are posted immediately to ledgers and used to produce statements and credit control documentation. Sales figures can be produced at the end of each month using the dealer codes shown on the invoices. Orders are put into a 'back-order' file so that they can be tracked; this task may be done perhaps once a day.

For a small company, invoicing may be carried out, say, twice a week and may only take an hour on the computer. Some files, such as the name and address file, may only need to be updated once a week. Monthly tasks include the payroll, and producing statements and accounts to be sent out.

This leaves the system free at other times for word-processing applications (letters and reports) and business planning. This software would also be integrated in a more comprehensive system.

In such a system, details on sales, expenditure, assets, liabilities and capital could be fed into a financial model from the nominal ledger. Various analyses could then be carried out, and management reports produced. Word-processing software could be used to add additional information and to improve the appearance of reports.

8

Manufacturing and Industrial Computing

Overview

Although most people are more aware of computers in retailing and commerce, the most marked effect of computers is in industry. As more industrial situations are computerised and processes automated, the numbers employed in the manufacturing sector falls, even with increased output. On the other hand the services sector is expanding to become the predominant employer of labour.

The modern manufacturing unit can demand a complexity of paperwork in its organisation and control. The application of computers can considerably simplify the problems of planning and control, thereby freeing the management to spend more time on decision making.

The direct application of computers to the plant and equipment is termed *process control*. With the development of microelectronics, it has become possible to have individual items of plant controlled locally by their own computer (or microprocessor built into the equipment) with perhaps several such units under the general control of a central computer.

The spread of robot applications is a particular example of this decentralised control. Prior to the development of microcomputers a robot would have a complex cable of wires connecting it to a large computer standing in the vicinity. The expense of such systems limited their economic application. Nowadays, with robots often costing less than a person, judged on normal investment criteria, it has become economic to construct complete factories with robots.

The systems that are designed and the products manufactured can also be designed by computers. The traditional design process can involve the engineers in a large amount of calculations. Often the calculations are iterative, that is, the calculation is done repeatedly, and each time the answer becomes more accurate. In practice, the cost of carrying out more than a few iterations would be prohibitive and so a less than ideal solution would be adopted. For example, a bridge would have to be designed deliberately too strong, to err on the safe side. A computer, by carrying out more iterations, can usually produce a design that meets the specification, but at the same time uses less materials.

A large part of a designer's time would be spent in producing the drawings. The lines on the plans would have to be positioned accurately and side views, top views, and so on would also have to be projected from the original view. The computer can take over this time-consuming activity, and free the designers for the more creative aspects of their work.

It is often desirable to experiment with the design of new systems or products. Many aspects of this experimentation can be carried out on a computer in *simulations* (see pp 116–21). Computer simulation may also be used to train new employees, as in the case of the operation of oil rigs. If the trainee makes a mistake on a computer model, little harm is done. A computer can also simulate proposed administrative changes, to aid management in determining the best policies to adopt.

Manufacturing systems

A manufacturing system can involve a mass of paperwork. The traditional works order system would include the paperwork issued and monitored by the Production Control Department as described below.

On receipt of an order, the Production Control Department would create Materials Requisition Slips that authorised the issue of sufficient materials from the stores. To do this they would have to consult Parts Lists, which contained details of what had to be produced to meet the order. Having identified individual parts that needed manufacturing, the Production Control Department would then have to consult the process planning documentation. This would tell them how much material to issue per item (taking into account a specified wastage rate), and would also give details of each stage of the production process, that is, the sequence of machines to be used, the time allowed per operation, and any inspection stages required.

When the above procedure is done manually, it results in a set of documents being produced for each order. This often meant that in order to clear it, the paperwork was issued as fast as it was raised. The effect of this was to have too much work going on at any one time, and due to congestion one job would delay another. In these circumstances the company would employ a team of progress chasers to urge the jobs that were late.

The typical manual Production Control system resulted in high work-in-progress and late deliveries. Computerisation was first applied, in the days of punched cards, to separating the original orders into their component parts, and producing the documentation for, typically, a week ahead. Thus computer updating runs would be done at the end of the week to provide an up-to-date work load for the start of the following week.

These Production Control systems helped reduce inventories and provided up-to-date reports of progress to management, but weekly control was still crude, as the actual situation was liable to change hourly. With the development of on-line systems, control was improved as the progressing and reporting periods shortened. However, there was one major factor that was not taken into account by these systems, namely the capacity of the individual processes. This would have increased the amount of information to be interrelated and processed beyond the capabilities of the computer systems. This has now changed with the availability of data bases. The Production Control systems nowadays have almost an unlimited scope to interrelate data and this has given rise to systems which have at their heart a Capacity Requirements Planning and a Materials Requirements Planning (MRP) module.

The modern system starts with a proposed Sales Program made up of firm orders and forecast orders. The implications of this are assessed by having the computer break down the orders into their required work load on machine centres and compare this to the centre's current capacity. The Sales Program is only finalised when it can be seen that it is feasible in the light of the current work load and available capacity. As a result of this stage, the need to sub-contract or work overtime and the cost implications, can be examined in advance.

The Materials Requirements Planning stage works backwards from the required delivery date, to determine when materials must be issued. In this way, work is not started before it is necessary, and therefore work-in-progress is reduced. Because the Materials Requirements Planning stage works right back to indicate when the raw material is required to be issued from stock, stock levels can be held at a minimum. Stock is bought in against a firm plan, not on the basis of topping up the shelves. A diagram of such a system is shown in Figure 8.1.

As the capacity of computer systems increases, the Production Control system can be integrated further with the Order Processing and Accounts systems to improve cash flow, with the Distribution

End item Master Schedule: Coffee Tables

Week no.	1	2	3	4	5	6	7	8
Requirements	30			40		40		30

Order quantity = 100
Lead time = 2 weeks

Component Material Plan: Table tops

	1	2	3	4	5	6	7	8
Projected requirements	30			40		40		30
Scheduled receipts						100		
On-hand at end of period	50	50	50	10	10	-30	70	40
Planned order release				100				

place order when negative

Order quantity = 400
Lead time = 1 week

Component Material Plan: Legs (4 off)

	1	2	3	4	5	6	7	8
Projected requirements	120			160		160		120
Scheduled receipts				400				400
On-hand at end of period	30	30	30	-130	270	110	110	-10
Planned order release			400				400	

place order when negative

Figure 8.1 An example of MRP

system to improve vehicle routing, and with Costing systems to improve management control.

Process control

The natural extension of using computers to control the organisational and administrative aspects of production is to use computers to control the plant and equipment. Over the years many items of plant and processes have been made more automatic, but computers allow far greater integration and control of the total process.

Computers can be used to control processes by means of *transducers*, that is, devices that can convert a non-electrical variable into electric signals, or vice versa. Transducers, in the form of sensors, can be used to monitor speed, temperature, weight, and so on, and pass this information back to a computer system. The computer can issue instructions in the form of electrical signals which, when passed to transducers designed as actuators, will stop a motor, close a valve, move a linkage, and so on.

An example of process control might be found in an agricultural animal feed mill. One typical mill produces about eighty different animal feedstuffs, with up to twenty ingredients per mix. A controlled quantity of raw material can be discharged as required from the appropriate hopper, and either directed into a mill (a machine to grind the raw material down to a specified particle size), or sent directly to a hopper which feeds the mixer. Output from the mixer is passed to another hopper, from where the mix is routed according to the bagging required.

As the cost of the raw materials varies from week to week, it is necessary to vary the ingredients in a mix to minimise costs while maintaining the nutritional balance. As well as this routine operation, the computer is used to facilitate opportunity buying of raw materials. Several times a week the mill will be offered raw materials at prices that can only be held for one or two hours.

A block diagram of the system of control is shown in Figure 8.2. One computer is used to develop the formulations, which can be accessed by the commercial director. The formulations developed by this computer are passed to another computer that controls the mill. The mill computer, in turn, passes details of stock used back to the commercial computer.

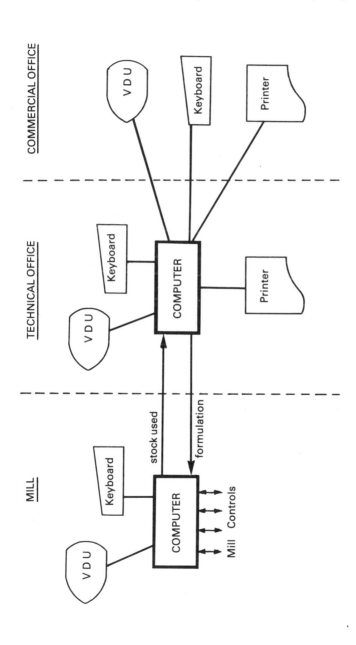

Figure 8.2 Process control of feedstuffs

Other industries

The principles of process control can be applied in many industries, for example, mining, cement, chemicals and paper making. In each case, the control system needs to be developed around the basic industrial technology that is used. Thus in mining, the monitoring and positioning of the cutting heads and the monitoring of environmental conditions are examples of the issues involved. In the cement industry, the monitoring of particle sizes and control of furnace temperatures are important. To achieve economies of scale in the production of chemicals, for example ammonia and ethylene, very large plants have been developed. The cost of a malfunction is prohibitive, and there is a need to reduce pollution and the use of energy as much as possible. All these requirements lead to an increase in the sophistication, and a greater degree of process control. The use of computers allows as much integration of the industrial process as required. The limitations are largely in understanding the process and the economics of implementing control procedures.

Computer Aided Design

Computer Aided Design (CAD) is a technique in which a computer is used to accept information from the designer, process and display it, and store results for subsequent loading and manipulation. The information may be entered by drawing on the computer's screen with a light pen, or on a digitising pad attached to the computer. Drawings may be output to a graph plotter, sometimes in colour.

The software supplied with CAD systems allows the designer to 'sketch' drawings or use functions for a more precise layout (for straight lines, arcs of circles, shading, and so on). The images can be rotated and translated to show the designer different views of the same object. Interactive controls, such as sophisticated joysticks, allow zooming in and magnification to display an enlarged version of part of the design. Parts of drawings, for example, the windows in a house, may be stored and called up when required. The software library may include a number of standard shapes, such as symbols for circuit diagrams and different typefaces.

In addition to these general types of drafting system, used basically for engineering drawing, software may be available for a particular CAD system that is aimed at more specific applications. For example, designers concerned with machines and their operatives may require software that incorporates a model of a man and standard shapes that can be built into three-dimensional models of, say, people sitting at work stations or working in the home or a driver sitting in a vehicle.

The model of the situation can be built interactively with the designer selecting options from a menu. Using simple commands, the designer can select different viewing points, and obtain three-dimensional views inside or outside of the model. The views may be in *wire form*, showing lines which would normally be hidden in real life. These hidden lines may be removed by the software to give a more realistic view, but since quite a lot of processing is involved in removing the lines, the response will be slower.

Another type of CAD software system may incorporate project information. When engineers design a complete plant in a process industry, such as a nuclear reactor plant, they have to consider where to locate many items of equipment and the layout of the necessary services, such as ducting for electric cables. Software is required for manipulating the design, performing stress calculations, and controlling the ordering of materials and project phases.

A data base is built up as the project progresses, containing details of components, items of equipment and layouts. The latter can be displayed on the screen, manipulated, and stored as updated versions in the data base. Various checks can be incorporated according to rules specified by the engineers and clashes with these identified. Another advantage is the availability of up-to-date information, stored in the data base, to all the engineers working on the project, thus ensuring consistency in the various parts of the design.

This type of CAD has been sponsored by the Department of Trade and Industry (DTI) under the CADCAM (Computer Aided Design/Computer Aided Manufacturing) programme, with the support of the Institution of Mechanical Engineers.

A parallel programme called CADMAT (Computer Aided Design Manufacturing and Test) has also been sponsored by the DTI, and further information can be obtained from the Institution of Electrical Engineers. This programme is concerned with using computer-aided techniques in the production of computers and electronic equipment.

For example, CAD techniques are used extensively in the production of microchips (integrated circuits). A microchip may consist of many layers of semiconductor material, such as silicon, separated by insulating layers of, say, silicon dioxide. Each layer has its circuit pattern engraved on it, and this is etched into the insulating material by a masking process known as *photolithography*.

Since a microchip may contain thousands of circuits, the masks are very complex. Special CAD software is available for automatically laying out the circuits, checking complex design rules (for example, spacing between lines and shapes), and modelling the integrated circuit to test that it will function as required.

Data may be generated as a by-product for manufacturing processes, for example, a punched paper tape may be produced by a CAD system and used to drive a photoplotter for drawing the circuits. Data may also be generated for testing the final product on automatic test equipment. The administrative tasks necessary for running the project may be controlled by a computer system, as described previously.

Industrial robots

Robots are used in industry for a variety of tasks which are repetitive and easily programmed. Some industrial robots are designed to move around the factory floor in a limited way, but most remain fixed in position.

A typical robot used in a manufacturing environment (see Figure 8.3) has a single arm that can move in three planes over a wide work area. Different 'hands' may be inserted at the 'wrist' end of the arm, for gripping different objects or for scooping up powders and liquids.

The hand may also be a tool for drilling, welding or spraying, or an electromagnet for picking up and dropping objects. Thin materials can be handled by using vacuum cups made of an elastic material. The vacuum seals can grip tightly without damaging the material, which is released quickly when the vacuum is broken.

In many industrial situations, robots are fitted with devices which

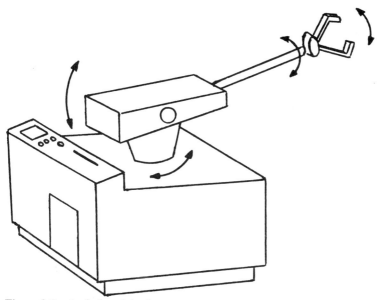

Figure 8.3 An industrial robot

enable them to select and move objects. These devices may be sensors which detect physical contact with objects (pressure-sensitive devices) or which respond to changes in a light beam (photoelectric devices) so that transparent and opaque objects can be distinguished. Inductive sensors can distinguish between objects having different magnetic properties, such as brass and steel.

Signals from the sensors are fed back to a computer for processing. The computer can then send a signal to the robot to cause it to move its arm and hand to grip the workpiece and lift it to the correct position, using electric or hydraulic power if necessary. Computers and various memories are available as single microchips, so that the computer controlling the robot's action is small enough to be placed inside the robot.

Programming of robots may be carried out by people who understand the actions required but have little computer experience, using special robot languages. Another way is to 'teach' the robot by physically moving it through the required cycle, and recording the movements as the 'program'.

It is possible to have automated factories controlled by robots under the supervision of one or two human operators, whose jobs may involve starting and setting up machines, and dealing with breakdowns. Using robots has a number of advantages, for example, whereas human operators need rest periods and can only work for limited shifts, robots can continue to work indefinitely, apart from non-productive periods (downtime) due to breakdowns or routine maintenance.

Human operators can work only in conditions that are not too hot or too cold, with sufficient space to move comfortably and with enough air and light. There are minimum working conditions which employers must provide for their employees. Robots, on the other hand, can be designed to work in extreme conditions, for example, in a narrow space and in a poisonous atmosphere.

The main limitations of robots are in their ability to 'see' and in the 'intelligence' that can be provided through computer programs. Extensive research is being carried out in these areas in several countries.

Investigations into stereo imaging techniques, using video cameras and optical pattern recognition, will lead to robots being able to select an object from a bin containing different industrial parts and orient it correctly for machining and assembly.

Research into artificial intelligence (AI) is leading to the design of more intelligent robots so that the signals coming in from sensors can be interpreted in a more human way. For example, a human operator can observe if something is going wrong, and quickly take corrective action. A robot has to be programmed to detect abnormal situations through its sensors, and the corrective action may be to shut the machine down or to send a warning message to the factory supervisor.

Robotics is a relatively new and expanding field with important applications in industry. For this reason many of the professional institutions are supporting investigations into robotics.

Simulation

Simulation is used in industry in two broad areas, to train people and to test out alternative ideas before making a decision. A flight simulator is an example of simulation methods being used to train pilots, while a simulation of lorries loading and unloading at a warehouse is an example of how the number of loading bays might be decided. Before discussing examples of simulation, a brief explanation of the principles will be given.

Everyone has probably been involved in a simulation although they may not have realised it. Many board games, such as *Monopoly*, are simulations. In *Monopoly*, the buying and development of property is simulated, and the winning of a prize is determined by drawing the appropriate card from the pack. In business simulations, the chance of an event occurring is represented more accurately, so that the consequences are more realistic, but there is less need for a physical model, such as the miniature token houses in *Monopoly*.

Many board games make use of dice to determine the move, for example, the need to throw a double six to get out of jail. In this case, the chance of getting out of jail is one thirty-sixth because there are thirty-six possible results from two dice. Some games, such as TSR Hobbies' *Dungeons and Dragons*, make use of more unconventional dice with eight, or twenty sides, etc. to simulate the 'odds' required by the rules. In industrial simulations, a computer can be used to select random numbers, as though a die had been thrown. Unlike using a conventional die, the computer is not restricted to selecting numbers between one and six. The instructions in the simulation program enable a computer to choose a number at random over any specified range. Thus if there is a one in ninety chance that a lorry will break down, the computer can, in effect 'throw' a ninety sided die to determine whether the lorry breaks down. When a simulated breakdown occurs, the computer can continue and select a further number at random to determine if the breakdown is due to a flat tyre, or some other reason. Quite complex situations can be simulated in this manner, the program sometimes being referred to as a *simulation model*.

The purpose of having a simulation model is to allow changes to be made in the model rather than in the real situation. In this way, alternative ideas can be tried out without making expensive mistakes or causing accidents in the real situation. Students of chemistry and scientists, studying industrial processes, experiment with a computer model so that if the simulated equipment 'blows up' no harm is done. Even when the changes could safely be made in the real situation, it may be quicker to use a simulation model. One year's operation of a stock control policy may be simulated within minutes on a computer so that the management do not have to wait a year to find out the consequences of a proposed change.

As an example of simulation, consider the following situation. A maintenance department has been maintaining an electric heat treatment oven for some years on the basis of changing elements as and when they fail. The Production Manager is now complaining that with the current work load he can't afford so much downtime.

When a single element is replaced it takes six days, including the cooling-down and re-heating time. The production manager argues that if one element has failed then the rest must be near the end of their lives and it would make better sense to change the whole lot, particularly as changing all six elements would not take six times as long, but only twelve days, that is, twice as long. The accountant, while seeing that the Production Manager's idea would increase the time the oven was available, is worried about the extra money that would be spent on replacement elements.

The above situation could be resolved by trying out the Production Manager's suggestion for a while and keeping records of the effect, but it could prove an expensive mistake. Alternatively, the situation could be simulated on a computer as follows.

An examination of past maintenance records would give details of the element breakdowns. If these were consolidated into a single chart, it would be possible to establish the chance of any element lasting, for example, 30 days, 35 days, and so on. Part of such a chart is shown in Figure 8.4.

The situation inside a hypothetical oven can now be simulated.

Life of element (days)	No of occasions	% chance	Cumulative %
-	-	-	-
-	-	-	-
25 -	40	2	78 - 79
30 -	60	3	80 - 82
35 -	40	2	83 - 84
40 -	20	1	85
-	-	-	-
-	-	-	-
TOTAL	2000	100	

Frequency 8.4   Frequency of element failure

The computer can generate a random number and relate this to the table in Figure 8.5, to simulate one of the six elements. If this is repeated six times, then the computer can set up in its memory an 'oven' which contains six typical 'elements' (see Figure 8.6).

Computer generated random number	Cumulative % (from Fig. 8.4)	Life of element (days)
	-	-
	-	-
79	78 - 79	25 -
	-	-
	-	simulated life
	-	-
	-	-

Figure 8.5 Allocation of random number

The next steps depend upon which maintenance policy is being simulated. Let us simulate the original policy, changing elements as and when they fail. As the computer 'knows' the lives of all the elements, it can identify which element will fail first. The life of this element determines the oven's running time. This element can be

Simulated element lives

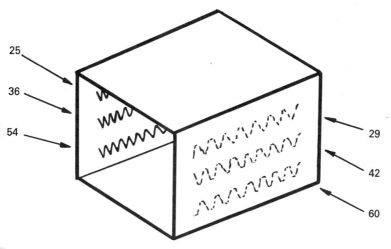

Figure 8.6 Hypothetical oven

'replaced' by a new one in the computer's memory by programming the computer under these conditions to select a 'new' element at random. Finally, the computer can subtract the running time from the lives of all the other elements to determine their remaining lives. A manual worksheet showing these steps is given in Figure 8.7.

OVEN ELEMENT NO						Running time	Downtime time
1	2	3	4	5	6		
25	36	54	29	42	60	25	6
	fails first replaced						
		(life remaining)					
49	11	29	4	17	35	4	6
45	7	25	52	13	31	7	6
				TOTAL		15640	1200

Figure 8.7   Manual worksheet

By repeating the above procedure several times, the computer can simulate the running and breakdown of the oven over a long period. When several thousand breakdowns have been simulated the computer can cost out the consequences of this policy. Figure 8.8 shows the nature of the calculations, if each element costs £50 to

```
Total no of elements used   =   200


Cost of elements        =   200 x 50    =   10000
Cost of downtime        =   1200 x 200  =   240000
                            Total cost      250000


Total running time      =   15640


Cost per running day    =   250000       =   £15.98
                            ──────
                            15640
```

Figure 8.8   Cost calculations

buy and instal, and it costs £200 a day to have the oven out of action.

Slight modifications of the program would allow the computer to simulate any other maintenance policies that were suggested. In this way, only better ideas would be implemented and costly mistakes would be avoided.

9

Home and Educational Computing

Overview

Prices of computer equipment have fallen dramatically in recent years, and with the development of the low-cost microcomputer there has been a rapid expansion in computing in schools and at home.

A range of low-cost microcomputers are available. These have facilities such as high resolution colour graphics, a reasonable amount of disk storage for word and data processing, inexpensive printers with upper/lower case and graphics characters, and interactive devices such as light pens and joysticks. In addition to this hardware, there is a range of software including programming languages for learning programming and developing usable software, and software packages for many different applications. It may be difficult to choose an appropriate system, but in the main, the choice will be based on the cost of the equipment and software, and on the facilities provided.

Schools tend to go for 'standard' equipment recommended by educational authorities. The advantages of this are compatibility between different schools to allow exchange of software, and the availability of financial support for some of the equipment. In addition, many schools have purchased equipment through their PTAs (Parent-Teacher Associations).

Computer applications in schools are varied and depend very much on the enthusiasm of the pupils and teachers. Sometimes the computer is only used as a club activity, but often the use of the computer is integrated into the curriculum. This is made easier if suitable software packages and supporting documentation is available.

Writing games software is a good educational exercise as it taxes the programmer's ingenuity, and involves reasoning and logic. Even using 'arcade' type games on a microcomputer can be educational, in that this can develop sensory and motor skills and may encourage students to start developing programs.

Just as computers in industry and commerce are used for data processing, the home or school computer can be used for simple record keeping. Files can be set up on cassettes or disks and processed to produce lists, labels, and so on.

Programming is time-consuming, and in many cases it is more important to use programs than to write them. A vast range of software is available on a commercial basis, and also from books, magazines and through exchange schemes. Programs may also be obtained through telesoftware schemes, as described in Chapter 4.

Selecting a home computer

When considering the price of a computer, extra costs need to be taken into account depending on the uses to which the computer will be put. For example, if the computer will be used to learn programming, then the basic machine using a cassette recorder for the storage of programs may be sufficient initially. However, advanced programming techniques include disk handling and the use of structured facilities. This will entail buying a disk drive, preferably a dual unit to make copying of disks and file processing easier; a printer for program listings and printed output, and perhaps another interpreter or compiler if you want to learn a different programming language (most microcomputers come with a BASIC interpreter).

There will be a continuous outlay on printer stationery, generally bought in boxes of about 1000 to 2000 sheets, and floppy disks, generally bought in boxes of 10. If cassettes are used, good quality audio cassettes are suitable, although computer stores also sell shorter playing-time cassettes of 12 to 15 minutes.

Compilers and interpreters are available for several different programming languages, such as FORTH and LOGO, which are described later in this chapter, and various versions of BASIC. The software may require extra circuit boards to give additional memory, or a second processor. An interpreter or compiler for a particular microcomputer may be supplied as a ROM chip, or as a ROM cartridge for plugging in externally, on disk or cassette tape.

With the software you should receive a user manual, perhaps with tutorial lessons. However, particularly if you want to go further than these lessons, you may need more books, and perhaps want to go on a course. Many courses in programming are offered by Colleges of Further and Higher Education. Some of these are intended as introductions to programming or applications, other courses are more advanced and require some experience, and may be oriented to particular types of equipment or software.

You may want to use your computer for 'real' applications such as word processing, home accounts or entertainment (games, music, graphics). The programs for these are likely to be complex, and you may prefer to buy ready-made packages available off the shelf in computer stores. Again, this software may come in ROM, on disk or cassette, and may require an upgrade of your machine.

For the more 'serious' applications, you may find that the software and upgrading costs are more than the cost of your original machine. It is, of course, essential to find out the exact machine configuration required for use with a particular piece of software. Questions to be asked include: how much memory, if it is used with disk or cassette, what is the disk format, if a second processor is required and what are the printer specifications. The problem of maintenance and associated costs is discussed separately later in the chapter.

Facilities
Within your price range, the availability of the facilities you require should be your first consideration. You will need to investigate what software you can run on your basic machine, what upgrades will be required, what peripherals are needed and if they are readily available. Often a manufacturer will market a basic machine and introduce extensions and upgrades at different stages. The programming language compilers and interpreters, and applications software may be marketed by different organisations. Computers may be purchased direct from manufacturers or through a variety of retail outlets which generally sell a range of equipment and software from different manufacturers.

The suitability of software for your purposes is difficult to assess.

Shops can provide demonstrations, but these are limited by how busy they are, and by the expertise of the sales person. Some experience and knowledge of particular software may be gained on college courses, at computer clubs and by reading reviews in computer magazines.

Maintenance

Home computing systems are based on modern computer technology which has high standards of reliability. In the main, if something is going to go wrong, this tends to happen during the first few months. After that you can expect occasionally to have problems with disk units and printers, but less frequently with the processor and memory boards, unless you are very unlucky. The manufacturer's guarantee may cover three, six or twelve months, and extended guarantees are available from some suppliers.

Maintenance contracts are available, but are generally not taken out for low-cost systems. They are based on an annual fee of about 10 to 15 per cent of the purchase price of the equipment, so you should allow about this amount for repairs. You may be able to purchase parts and repair the equipment yourself if, say, just a chip has blown, but usually it is better to take the equipment back to the supplier if something goes wrong. Disk drives, in particular, need special equipment to set them up correctly, and expensive test equipment, such as logic analysers, may be required to detect faults and for checking circuitry.

Future requirements

New computers and software are continually coming on the market and you may feel that your equipment will quickly become obsolete. You can take the attitude that your first computer is for gaining an introduction to computing and will then have served its purpose, so that you can move on to a better, more expensive machine.

On the other hand, you may want to look for a computer that can be expanded to provide many more facilities. With some computers you can expand the memory, add more peripherals, add a second processor, and link the computer to other small computers or to large information retrieval systems. This expansion in hardware may then make possible the use of a further range of software – programming languages and applications.

Games

The home computer market has developed out of the tremendous interest in computer games. As the number of games have increased, so has the justification for buying a home computer rather than a specialised games machine. The range of games is continually expanding, and can be compared to the pop music scene. Some games writers have become so well known that their latest games immediately attract attention and are extensively reviewed. Some software houses have achieved reputations for consistently good games and have a similar following. One or two games have been so successful that they have been developed into a series with a consistent theme or character.

Arcade-type games

Early computer games were imitations of successful arcade games. Perhaps the first game to capture the public imagination and become well known was 'Space Invaders'. This game is a typical invader game and is responsible for generating a whole range of similar games. At first, the home computer versions of the arcade games were cruder, but now there is little to choose between dedicated arcade machines and home computer versions of a game. The difference is due largely to economic factors rather than the capability of the microcomputer. Home computers are usually used with the domestic TV set whereas the arcade game employs a high quality monitor. Arcade machines will continue to lead the way due to the investment involved, but home computers can follow.

The features of arcade games are good graphics, fast action and realistic sound. These features are therefore expected in similar home computer games. High resolution graphics on a computer takes up a lot of memory. As the cost of memory comes down, home computers with larger memories become possible, and they are able to support high resolution displays in games. More programming effort is required to develop high resolution displays, but as they become the norm, any arcade style game must incorporate them if it is to sell.

An example of how some home computers have developed facilities to increase the sophistication of the screen display is given by the provision of *sprite* facilities. When a computer uses high resolution graphics on the screen, the computer's memory stores details of what is to be displayed in every cursor position. A sprite facility allows additional screen areas to be defined in the memory, and displayed as required on the screen. The effect is that a sprite design can be superimposed onto an existing high resolution screen display and moved around independently by programming logic. The sprite may be displayed over or under the existing screen display.

One popular micro, the Commodore 64, allows sprites to be designed within a 21 by 24 block of dots, as shown in Figure 9.1. Eight different sprites can be designed and displayed on the screen simultaneously, and thus very elaborate screen displays can be created.

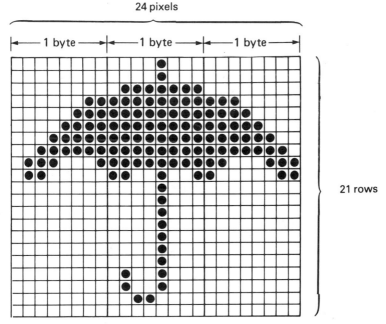

Figure 9.1 Sprite design for an umbrella

Although the provision of sprite facilities was brought about by the requirements of games, they can be used in other applications. For example, sprites can be designed as messages which pop up over an existing screen display without destroying it.

Fast action and fast response times are more related to the programming language used. The language traditionally associated with the home computer is BASIC. While this is a suitable choice for novice programmers, it is too slow for arcade type games. Arcade type games are usually written in machine code or a specialised language such as FORTH (which is described later in this chapter). Advertisements for such games often stress their speed by mentioning that they are written in machine code.

When playing a fast action game, it can be found that using a keyboard slows up the player's response. For this reason it is very common to use joysticks with an arcade style game. In addition to the computer manufacturer's 'authorised' joystick, there are many designs of joysticks available from specialist manufacturers. A responsive joystick makes all the difference between an average and a record score.

Because arcade games require a high degree of skill, there are several levels of play. The novice can start on the lowest level, and progressively work up to the higher levels as their skill increases. Some games have over thirty levels! This also ensures that the game will retain its attraction for a long time, even for a quick learner. In addition to playing arcade games competitively with others, many people compete against themselves, trying to beat their best score to date. Most games therefore display the highest score in addition to the current score.

Space Invaders has been mentioned as an example of the early arcade game. The development of this style of game has given rise to a range of science fiction, space age shoot-out games. Another range of games are based on being chased round a maze. As the software market grows, the variations of arcade games continues to develop, but in all cases the emphasis is on fast action on the screen calling for quick responses from the player.

Simulation games

Another type of game that is in some ways suited to computerisation is the *adventure game*. The traditional adventure game is played by a group of people, each having a collection of characters who undertake a joint expedition. The expedition can be set in a maze of dungeons or across unfamiliar lands. The objective of the game is usually to find treasure, and in their wanderings the expedition meets a range of fantasy creatures. The rules of the traditional adventure games are very open-ended, and usually an umpire (dungeon master) is used to plan the scenario, interpret the rules, and generally mastermind the game. The success of the game largely depends upon the management of the adventure by the umpire. However, it can take a long time for the umpire to interpret and arbitrate during the game, and so the pace can be slow.

In many ways a home computer is ideal for adventure games. The computer, acting as umpire, is much quicker at making decisions. Also, you can play an adventure game on a computer by yourself, you don't have to arrange to meet with a group of friends. On the other hand, serious adventure gamers would argue that the inter-personnel relationships of a joint expedition and the open-endedness of the rules made possible by using a human umpire are the most important features of an adventure. In simulating an adventure on a home computer, the game becomes very con-strained by the programming logic. Thus a computer may at a certain stage only allow the player four courses of action, whereas a human umpire would consider any suggestion and judge it on its feasibility.

The success of a computer adventure game is therefore depen-dent on the ingenuity of the programmer. Although they cannot replace the traditional adventure game, they do have advantages for the individual adventurer. Because of the inbuilt constraints, the computer adventure game becomes more of a puzzle solving game whereby the correct course of action needs to be found. Due to the limitations of a computer to accept free style English, an instruction to the computer can be met with a standard 'I do not understand' response, for example, 'Pick up mirror' may not be recognised, but 'Get mirror' may be accepted. A lot of time can be spent trying alternative phrases which mean essentially the same thing.

Some adventure games are played completely with text messages and responses whereas others use graphics to display the situation. Text-based adventures can be more complex, but require the players to use their imagination. Younger players are more likely to prefer the graphic adventures. Adventure games can take many hours to complete, and so it is usual to have a *save situation* facility, so that the game can be continued at a later date without having to start from the beginning.

Variations of the adventure game can simulate a wide range of realistic situations. A common simulation, available for most microcomputers, is an aircraft flight simulation. Typically, you are required to land an aircraft using the instrumentation displayed on the screen. The more sophisticated of these games also show a 3-D view from the cockpit.

War gaming

One type of gaming simulation, that had a large following before microcomputers became popular, and lends itself to computerisation is war gaming. War games are run very much like adventure games, except that the scenario is based as closely as possible upon realistic situations. Often the war game is a recreation of a historical battle, but they can be hypothetical situations. The comments made about adventure games largely apply to computerised wargames, that is, they tend to be more restrictive than a traditional wargame. An important, if not the most important, aspect of a war game is the management of your forces. Although a computerised war game is likely to provide you with a number of screen reports, it is still largely up to the player to organise the information available. This is a reflection of your competence as a commander and it is therefore up to you to decide what additional charts, maps, tables, and so on, are needed.

Traditional games

A range of traditional games are available on microcomputers. The attraction of playing these types of game on a computer is that you need never lack an opponent, as you can play against the computer. In addition, if the games offer you levels of play, you can gradually build up your skill.

The classic of traditional games, Chess, is the most widely available. Other games such as Backgammon, Draughts, Nim, Othello, Scrabble, and several card games are also readily available.

One of the consequences of computerising these types of game is that the strategy of the game has had to be closely analysed. This means that with Chess, for example, the standard of play by the computer has steadily increased as better strategic algorithms have been developed. Most microcomputers should be able to beat the average chess player when played at the highest level.

Chess games usually allow the player to choose their colour. Moves are entered via the keyboard using standard chess algebraic notation. Some chess programs contain a *hint* function which suggests the next move if required. Chess, however, is a complex game, and even with the speed of microcomputers the computer can take a long time to work out its next move. Depending upon the level of play, the computer's response may be anything from instantaneous to an hour or more.

Other features of chess games might include the ability to swop sides at any stage, and the means of saving a game. Swopping sides can be very instructive if you want to see how the computer would get you out of your currently hopeless position. Saving a game can be useful for the higher level, longer running game as you can play it over several days. The ability to replay a game in single steps is also useful for analysis. This feature is often linked to the ability to set up a position from a textbook and start from that stage.

Games such as Backgammon are similarly highly developed, but word games such as Scrabble are harder to implement. This is because this type of game is very dependent on having an extensive dictionary in its memory. The content of the dictionary not only determines the level at which the computer can play, but also which words it will recognise and accept from the player.

In many ways, one can argue that these games are the modern equivalent of patience for the individual who has a microcomputer available.

Practical 'games'

There are a variety of programs that, while not exactly games, may be used mainly for amusement. The type of programs in question are represented by astrology and biorhythm applications. The feature of these applications is that a large amount of calculations are involved to produce the output. A home microcomputer is ideal for this purpose, so that a person interested in these areas can forget the technicalities and concentrate on the interpretation of the output.

Other types of program with a similar 'practical' entertainment value are those that analyse your lifestyle, in response to a series of answers to questions, and state for example, 'you should take more exercise'.

The degree to which you treat these programs as pure entertainment depends on how seriously you regard the topic. If you are a serious believer in astrology, for example, then you would need to investigate the basis of the programming involved before accepting the output. The same applies to a health guide program or personality test.

Charts and diagrams

The graphics capability of home computers can be usefully exploited to produce charts and diagrams rather than just output results in tabular form. Regardless of the particular display required, there are a number of general considerations that need to be taken into account when developing charting and diagrammatic routines. Often standard programs are available as utilities for this stage of an application.

The degree of detail possible in a chart depends upon the resolution available with a particular microcomputer. This is partly related to the number of characters per line and the number of lines on the screen. For example, if a screen is 40 characters wide by 25 lines deep and a character is built up from a pattern of 8 by 8 dots (or pixels), then the resolution of the screen is 320 by 200 dots. Some microcomputers allow the user to select a resolution mode to suit the application. Bar charts might not demand high resolution, whereas plotting of mathematical functions, for example, $y = \sin(x)$, usually needs the highest resolution possible, because the objective is to make the function appear as a continuous line.

Another factor to be considered in charting routines is the flexibility in labelling the axes and headings. Ideally, the routine should be able to scale the chart automatically, yet even when automatic routines are used, the choice of scale intervals is sometimes unsatisfactory and so a manual override is desirable. Similarly, headings might always be displayed in a fixed position that under some circumstances blots out the underlying data. Ideally, it should be possible to specify where the headings are to be displayed. One spreadsheet package that has a plotting facility allows the user to display a heading on the screen, and then to move it around the screen to any desired position.

When charts are displayed on the screen, it is useful to be able to compare one chart with another. This has led to software allowing the user to split the screen into two sections so that different information can be displayed in each screen area.

If the results are particularly interesting, it is useful to be able to print them out. A sophisticated software package will allow the user to specify the codes necessary to work with a range of printers. Without this type of option, the user is tied down to using one particular printer.

A further consideration with charting routines or packages is the degree of control the user has over the colours displayed. Certain colour combinations may appear best for a particular television set; using a black-and-white set restricts the choice still further. Lastly, if printouts are required, the manner in which the printer responds to a coloured display needs to be investigated.

Types of charts

The simplest type of chart to display is the *bar chart*. The bars may be displayed horizontally or vertically. Depending upon the application, the bar chart, particularly if displayed vertically, may be called a *histogram*. An example of a histogram, produced on a microcomputer, is shown in Figure 9.2.

High resolution plots of mathematical functions enable graphs to be displayed. The accuracy and general quality of the plot depends upon the resolution possible with the particular microcomputer and screen being used, as mentioned above. Graphs may also be plotted from data values, either held in the program, input via the keyboard, or read from data files. This is a common method for business applications where the graph might be a set of sales figures, for example.

In scientific applications (which may include sales forecasting), the plot is often of a mathematical function, or combinations of functions. A home computing example may be found in a Biorhythms package, where it is required to plot and superimpose three cosine functions. Another example would be found in packages that draw simple geometric shapes on the screen. More complex packages allow three dimensional shapes to be built up. This is the basis

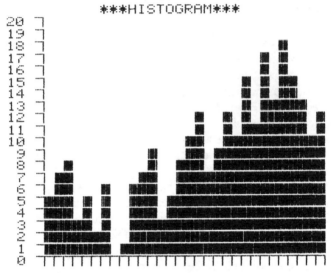

Figure 9.2   A histogram

of computer-aided design (CAD) as discussed in Chapter 8.

A commonly used chart, the *pie chart*, is an example of plotting a circular function and then shading in the desired segments. Although this chart is simple in concept, it is an example of a graphing requirement on the computer that requires a lot of programming. For this reason, graphics utilities are a very useful adjunct to the basic programming facilities, particularly as the average programmer may not have sufficient familiarity with the mathematics involved.

Record keeping

The principles of data processing were explained in Chapter 5. Some of these can be applied even on home computers which only have a cassette recorder for storing data. However, it is much more useful to have a disk unit to simplify the updating procedure.

Processing of club membership records is a good example of the sort of record keeping that can be done on a home computer. Figure 9.3 shows the data entry screen layout for this application.

Each record is given a unique number, then the name, address

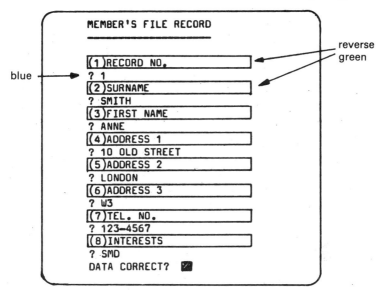

Figure 9.3   A data entry screen layout

and telephone number is entered, followed by a code for the interests of the member (for example, SMD indicates an interest in sports, music and drama). All this data is entered directly from the keyboard, so the screen has been designed to make it easy to use, with an option of correcting any line of data at the end. When Y or YES is entered in reply to DATA CORRECT?, the record can be stored on cassette tape or preferably on disk, since at a later stage it is likely that the information will need to be updated (for example, if a member moves to a new address).

Apart from the data entry and updating programs, further programs could be written to produce reports such as a list of names and telephone numbers of club members who are interested in sports, music, or drama, and a complete list of names and addresses placed in alphabetic order. These could be displayed on the screen or printed out as 'hard-copy' reports if a printer is attached to the computer. A printer is also useful for producing labels for sticking onto envelopes; special printer stationery is available which has self-adhesive labels stuck on it. The labels can easily be peeled off after printing the names and addresses, and then put on envelopes.

Computing in schools

Computers in schools are mainly used for teaching programming, to control models and laboratory equipment, as educational tools in different disciplines including geography, science and history, and for word and data processing. Games are also useful for familiarising pupils with computers; educational quizzes can be made interactive and more fun to use by using a light pen or joystick for selecting options on the sort of screen layout shown in Figure 9.4.

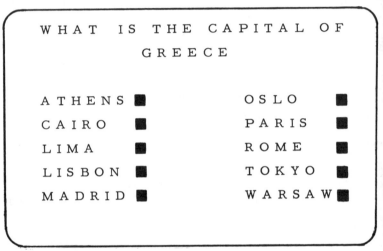

Figure 9.4   Screen layout for a quiz

Software packages are available from several sources, such as MEP (Microelectronics Education Programme) and MUSE (Microcomputer Users in Schools and Education). The programs should be provided with good documentation, including notes for teachers and workbooks or exercises for students.

Turtle graphics

In primary schools, the computer is proving useful in encouraging children to learn arithmetic and spelling, and to acquire general knowledge, and helping them to gain an idea of measurement and shapes.

The concept of turtle graphics (simulating a 'turtle' moving over the screen from point to point) and the language LOGO were invented by Seymour Papert in the USA. Various implementations of LOGO allow quite young children to draw shapes on the screen using simple commands. For example, in one version of LOGO, a square of side 30 'units' can be drawn on the screen by just entering FORWARD 30 (or FD 30) and RIGHT 90 (or RD 90), to turn a right angle, four times.

An extension to the screen displays is the use of a computer-controlled device (a turtle) which moves over a piece of paper to draw the shapes as the commands are entered into the microcomputer to which it is attached. Several devices of varying price and complexity are on the market for linking to different microcomputers. A sketch of a turtle is shown in Figure 9.5.

Control applications

For older pupils, computer-controlled lifts, cranes, and so on, can be used to teach control applications. Simple models can be constructed from wood, metal and plastics, so that through an interdisciplinary approach of craft and design technology, electronics and programming, many aspects of computer control can be explained and demonstrated.

A model of a simple lift is shown in Figure 9.6. This has a wooden frame on which a motor, lights (light-emitting diodes, LEDs) and push-button switches are mounted. A block of balsa wood is mounted on a central shaft and is driven up and down by the motor. The controls for the lift have to be mounted on the wooden frame to simulate the panel that would in reality be inside the lift.

Lines from an input/output port, which is a microchip connected to an 'edge' connector at the back of a microcomputer, are connected to the lights; to switches (including the microswitches at the top and bottom of the frame which limit the extent of travel of the lift); to the motor controls (start/stop, reverse), and to the Hall Effect integrated circuits (which detect when the lift has reached a particular floor).

The program that controls the lift is written in a version of BASIC that allows the input/output port to be 'addressed'. Although the logic of the program is fairly complex, BASIC is quite fast enough, as the lift moves slowly. The program detects when the lift is at a particular floor and moves it up or down, according to the requests

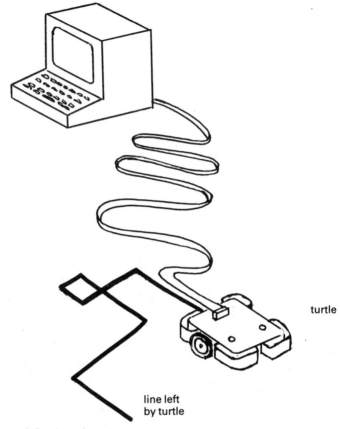

Figure 9.5   A turtle

received from the push-button switches at the floors or on the lift panel. The lights show which switches have been pressed.

Another application could be controlling the heating of water. The temperature of the water could be measured by a sensor called a *thermocouple*, which is made up of two dissimilar metals. A temperature change at the junction of the two metals causes a change in the voltage output from the thermocouple circuit. The output from the thermocouple can be linked to a computer to control the heating circuits.

A computer can only accept digital signals that are set to one of

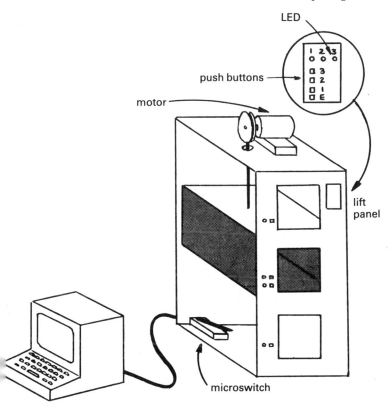

Figure 9.6　A computer-controlled model lift

two conditions – high or low voltages (such as 5 volts or 0 volts) to represent a binary 1 or 0. Thermocouples give a continuous voltage output, known as an *analog signal*, and this needs to be converted to a digital signal before putting it onto the input/output port of the computer. This may be done using an analog to digital (A/D) converter. Some microcomputers have A/D converters built in that can be used for this sort of purpose.

Constructing models may be too time-consuming for some students who wish to concentrate on the programming aspects. For these students, the use of commercially-available equipment, such as robot arms and computer-controlled trolleys, may be more appropriate. These usually come with some software but also provide scope for further programming.

Programming languages used with microcomputers

The main programming language used with microcomputers is BASIC. The version of BASIC used depends on which micro-computers are available.

Many schools now use BBC microcomputers, which use a version of BASIC that has the REPEAT . . . UNTIL command, and also named procedures (subroutines) so that structured programming techniques can be used. Other commands such as MOVE, DRAW and PLOT allow graphics to be programmed in various resolutions depending on the screen mode selected. There are also facilities for programming sound. Colour graphics and sound are available with most popular microcomputers, such as the Commodore 64 which also has a music synthesiser.

Another language that is popular in schools which obtained their computers before the BBC machine came on the market, is called COMAL (see p. 36). This has some of the structured facilities available in Pascal, including the CASE command which allows the programmer to list options and their outcome, so that depending on which condition is true, the appropriate result will be executed by the computer.

BASIC is suitable for many applications such as the simple record keeping described earlier. BASIC is quite fast enough for this type of application, which gives students some idea of commercial data processing as well as providing useful exercises in programming.

However, some control and graphics applications require a fast response from the computer. Programs for these may need to contain routines written in machine code or assembler, which will be much faster than the equivalent BASIC routines. Another language, FORTH, is about half the speed of machine code and is becoming a popular alternative for fast processing.

FORTH was invented by Charles Moore, around 1972, for controlling the observatory where he worked as an astronomer. FORTH is said to be a programming language, compiler and operating system, all in one. It has a number of elementary words that can be built up into more words for particular functions. This means that a complete subroutine can be defined as one word and used as such in another routine. This can make FORTH difficult to read, but it is possible to structure a FORTH program and include plenty of comments so that it can be understood by another programmer.

The main advantage of using FORTH, where fast processing is required, is that programs can be developed quickly since each word can be tested as it is designed. FORTH programs are compact because they are *compiled* into machine code.

FORTH has been used extensively not only for control applications, but also for business applications and games where graphic displays are used and a very fast interactive response is essential.

Computer Assisted Learning

Computer Assisted Learning (CAL) is a technique in which the computer is used with special programs to teach particular areas of specific knowledge.

Information and questions are displayed on the screen; the student's replies are checked by the program and suitable responses are in turn displayed to indicate how well the student is progressing; a score may be displayed and also stored for the student's supervisor.

The advantages are that the students can work as slowly or as quickly as they wish, repeat material, and get immediate feedback on their response to questions. A well-designed program with attractive displays can make learning fun and can result in faster progress for some students. CAL has been investigated extensively in the UK through the Council for Educational Technology (CET).

Special 'author' languages are available that allow teachers and trainers to develop material without acquiring computing and programming expertise, and which enable students to respond to questions displayed on the computer's screen in as natural a way as possible.

PILOT is an example of this type of language, and is available on a variety of microcomputers. Figure 9.7 shows an extract from a program written in a version called Tiny PILOT.

Tiny PILOT allows four main operation codes to be used for:

```
11   *Q2
12   T;WHAT IS THE NAME OF THE LAW THAT
13   T;RELATES VOLTAGE TO CURRENT AND
14   T;RESISTANCE IN THE FOLLOWING
15   T;RELATIONSHIP.  V = I * R
16   T;
17   A;
18   T;
19   M;GIVE UP
20   TY;OHM'S LAW
21   JY;*Q3
22   M;OHM
23   TN;NO. TRY AGAIN. THE LAW IS ASSOCIATED
24   TN;WITH THE NAME OF A PERSON
25   TN;
26   JN;*Q2
27   M;OHM'S LAW
28   TN;ALMOST RIGHT.  AS IT IS NAMED AFTER
29   TN;A PERSON IT IS OHM'S LAW
30   TY;CORRECT.
31   *Q3
```

Figure 9.7   A PILOT program

Displaying text (T);
Accepting input from the user and storing this as an answer in the computer's memory (A);
Matching text against the stored answer (M);
Jumping to a 'label' in a different part of a program (J).

Conditional modifiers are Y (for a successful match) and N (for a mismatch), shown as TN and TY in the program.

In the example in Figure 9.7, the student is given the formula for Ohm's Law and is asked for the name of the law. Each reply is tested against the correct answer. If the reply does not match, various responses can be programmed according to the type of reply from the student.

Another version called Common PILOT allows misspelling to be anticipated in two ways. If it is felt that an individual letter may be incorrect, the 'match text' can contain an asterisk, for example:

M; COMPUT*R

This would allow the user to respond with 'COMPUTER', 'COMPUTOR', or 'COMPUTUR', and still obtain a match. When a response may have some of the letters correct, but several wrong, & can be used, for example:

M; DI&P&Y

This anticipates that the correct response, DISPLAY, may be misspelt. The ampersand allows any number of incorrect letters between the specified text.

PILOT software systems contain a variety of editing features similar to those associated with word processing. For example, lines can be deleted or inserted, and the lines are automatically renumbered. New hardware developments will result in a much wider range of information being taught through CAL. For example, video-disc players may be linked to a computer. This allows pictures and sound to be generated through the computer from the disc. Special software can overlay or intersperse the pictures with text, and find particular frames.

Sources of programs

To make full use of a computer in the home or in schools, it is essential to have access to the appropriate software. Commercially available software is advertised in most of the widely-read computer magazines. These magazines also publish listings of programs which have been written by readers and can be keyed in to the appropriate computer.

A number of organisations have initiated software exchange schemes which provide free or low-cost programs to members; these are mainly games, utilities and educational programs.

Computer clubs and user groups are a useful means of gaining and exchanging knowledge, and these again are publicised in computer magazines. Another useful feature of belonging to a club or user group is the possibility of having discounts on equipment from some suppliers.

Micronet 800

Micronet 800 is a service available via Prestel (see Chapter 4) that allows microcomputer users to download information. The home microcomputer is connected by means of a modem to the telephone. Acoustic couplers and modems are available for most common microcomputers and, depending on the model, the appropriate leads, hardware and software are provided as a 'Networking Interface'. The hardware may include a special graphics chip to upgrade the microcomputer for this type of application. In some cases the user can choose to have the software supplied on cassette or disk.

There is a quarterly charge for the Micronet 800 service in addition to the Prestel quarterly charge. However, when the system is used during the evening or at weekends, there is no 'computer connect' charge, and the telephone charge is usually at local call rates. A subscriber receives a Micronet 800 directory every quarter, and is allocated a password to access Micronet 800.

Micronet 800 allows a microcomputer to be used in a variety of ways. Free games can be downloaded from the *Aladdin's Cave*, or others downloaded at a discounted price. These programs include educational software and business applications. Competitions are also run, with prizes. User groups for the major manufacturers supply news and reference information. Clubs run 'bulletin boards' of news, events and swap-shops. A 'mailbox' service is offered whereby messages can be exchanged between users.

Because Micronet 800 users are automatically Prestel users, they can access the 250000 pages of Prestel that include news, travel, holiday and entertainment information. If required, they can use their microcomputer to make bookings.

Micronet 800 allows schools and educational establishments to exchange information and programs. Micronet 800 also has closed areas that allow business users to send information to outlets and branches, or to their salesmen and engineers working from home.

10

Impact of Computers

Overview

The widespread use of computers has resulted in data being stored in computer files on many different subjects. Much of commerce is based on computer-held information, some of which is personal data on individuals. It is important that the individuals concerned know what information is held on them to ensure that this is correct.

Access to personal data and to industrial information needs to be restricted, so that only certain people are authorised to view or change the information. Techniques have been developed to control access to information by both hardware and software. This control is easier to achieve on larger computer systems in which the operating system has facilities for checking a user's authorisation and access codes. On smaller computers without these facilities, care has to be taken over the storage of disks and tapes to prevent unauthorised use.

Several countries have devised legislation to ensure privacy of information. Transfer of information between countries may be inhibited if one of the countries does not have appropriate data protection legislation. This can severely restrict an organisation's activities, and hence this type of legislation has become essential for major trading countries.

Data files may be destroyed through physical hazards, or failures in hardware and software. Techniques are available for ensuring that recovery can take place after a failure; some of which can be applied to microcomputer systems.

The use of computers in industry, commerce, hospitals, schools and the home is having a wide impact on very many people, including the disabled. Issues such as the effect on employment, implications for health care, and the wider availability of education to create new opportunities have come to the fore.

Various organisations have set up schemes to promote investigations in Information Technology. The aims are to make potential users aware of the uses and limitations of computers, and to create new systems.

Controlling access to information

On a time-sharing system, where many users share the use of the central processor and peripherals via terminals, the first security measure is the identification of users who are authorised to have access to the computer system.

To use the system, the user keys in a unique code, which is checked by the operating system against a list held in the computer. The user will only be allowed access to the system if the code matches one on the list. The code may also be used for accounting purposes when users are charged for processor and peripheral time.

Further information may be recorded against each user code to limit the type of usage, such as access only to certain files according to an access level number, and the amount of disk storage allocated for programs and data. A programmer may need a large disk storage area for program development and test files, whereas a business user may only use shared programs and files.

It is useful to be able to set a time limit on any programs run by the user, in case a program gets into an endless loop when after a time it will be automatically stopped by the operating system. Similarly, a limit on the amount of printed output produced can control the situation further when a program has gone wrong.

In a time-sharing system, it is useful to be able to allocate execution priority levels, either to the user or to the program. This ensures that programs of higher priority are run before those of lower priority. In some systems, the peripherals that a user can access are controlled by an access code. This allows limited use of some special printers and graph plotters, for example.

These controls help the computer system to run smoothly by allocating computer resources according to user needs, as well as limiting access for security purposes.

Passwords may also be used for additional security to prevent access to the computer system, files, records or items within data bases. The user may be allocated a password, in addition to an account code, or users may be able to set their own passwords. Passwords need to be kept secret and not printed or displayed on the terminal, unless they are overprinted or masked. Also, they should be changed frequently for greater security.

Access to many commercial systems is through the telephone via modems. The user needs to know the dialling code for the computer, an account number, and perhaps passwords. Unauthorised users may try to gain access to information for illegal purposes and various techniques have been devised to prevent and detect fraudulent use of a system.

For example, attempts to break into the system by trial and error methods can be detected by recording each entry type, time of day, terminal used, and user, when logging in and out of the system, including whether a correct or incorrect password was given. This information can be checked by the organisation's security officer and users, so that they can check the use that has been made of their files. Wide publicity should be given of the existence of such a security system, to deter unauthorised users from attempting to break into the computer system.

A technique known as *cryptography* may be used to conceal information stored in the computer (such as passwords or sensitive data) or during transmission over telephone lines (in case the lines are tapped).

Commonly used methods encode the information so that it cannot be read without the key for decoding it. The transformation of the information may be carried out by software or hardware. Sophisticated methods tend to be costly, and are used especially for sensitive data.

The main measures that can be taken for stand-alone microcomputers are clearing information from the computer's screen and memory after using it, and locking disks and tapes away. A log should be kept of the information held on numbered disks and tapes, when they are used, by whom, and for what purpose.

Data protection legislation

The increase in information processing activity has created more complex problems in ensuring the accuracy of computer files, and limiting access to information contained in them. Large organisations, in particular, may have personal data stored on many small computers as well as on the central data base. An example is a local authority where computers are used in various departments, schools and colleges. The processing of personal data, its use, and access to it by individuals has to be controlled according to the requirements of data protection legislation. Each country has its own regulations, so only some general principles are discussed here.

Registration

All data processing systems in an organisation holding personal data, including main computers, microcomputers and word processors, need to be registered with a Registrar. The registration includes such details as purposes for which the system is to be used; the data held on it; any linkages to other systems involving transfer of, or access to, personal data; how long the data is to be held (retention time); who will use the data, and when it will be used. Organisations must also provide adequate back up of data files, and state the security measures for restricting access to the data.

The register is made available to the general public and individuals can request to see information held on them in particular data files; a fee may have to be paid for this service. The organisation then has a duty to supply this information in a form that is intelligible to the individual. This is important as much of the information may be held in coded form in the computer files.

The Registrar has to ensure that registered organisations comply with the legislation. Possible sanctions against organisations not fulfilling their obligations include fines and de-registration, resulting in transfer of information being prohibited.

This is the basis of the type of data protection legislation which has the following purposes. As well as ensuring the free flow of information between countries, the intention of such legislation is to establish the principle that personal information held on computer files can be inspected and corrected by the individuals concerned as a right, with some exceptions, for example, in the case of national security.

Reliability of systems

The reliability of computer systems is a prime consideration as loss of important information and programs always causes great inconvenience for users, and can be very expensive for a company. Failure may occur in various parts of the computer system. However, some sort of service may still be available to users although this may be degraded (i.e. the response at the terminals may be slower, or certain files may not be accessible).

If the central processor fails, then the computer system cannot function unless there is a second processor to which work can be switched. If a VDU fails, so that there is no display, or wrong characters are displayed, then a spare terminal may be used. Similarly, output can be switched to an alternative printer, in some cases, if one fails.

Failure of disk drives can cause problems, particularly for microcomputers having only one disk drive. Most commercial systems have at least two disk drives, to make file copying easier, and to extend the amount of on-line disk storage.

Some hardware failures can be dealt with quickly. For example, if part of the memory fails, the service engineer can identify which memory board or microchip failed, and replace it. A disk drive failure, shown up as a misread of a record, may be caused by dirt on the read/write heads, and may be cured by cleaning them.

Large computer systems are maintained regularly by highly-trained computer service engineers on weekly or monthly visits. The engineers may spend a whole morning or afternoon checking through the system using special software, cleaning disk drive heads, and so on. This type of preventive maintenance makes systems much more reliable.

System failure

Despite these measures, the systems will fail occasionally. When this happens, the service engineer will be called out, and should arrive at the installation within a short time, depending on the terms of the maintenance contract. Some installations have resident engineers. The fault may be located using diagnostic software, in some cases, through an on-line link to the manufacturer's service centre. Service contracts are available also for microcomputer systems, either on site, or by taking the equipment to the service centre.

Software failure

Software can be the cause of failure. For example, a program could cause wrong data to be recorded on a disk, or even delete a disk file accidentally. Software failures are minimised by testing all programs, whether written in-house or purchased, with suitable test data before going 'live'.

Mishandling of equipment

A third type of failure can be caused through mishandling of equipment or media by the people using it. In a commercial system, tapes and disks holding data files and programs are under the control of a tape/disk librarian. The operators using the system are trained in handling disks and tapes, and other equipment in the computer room or in offices. In addition, procedures are set up for backing-up files (taking copies) so that no information is lost if a failure occurs.

For small disk files, a complete copy of the file can be created on disk or tape, so that if a subsequent run goes wrong, the previous file can be loaded and updated again. The file copies, of data and programs, should be kept separately, preferably in a fire-proof safe.

Special techniques are required for larger data bases. When these are updated, the transactions (data additions, deletions and amendments) are logged onto a magnetic disk or tape. The data base itself is partially copied (dumped) onto disk or tape at regular intervals, so that it can be reconstructed if failure occurs and the current data base is corrupted or destroyed. The log files are used to bring the last complete version of the data base up to date by replacing or correcting data items.

Effect on employment

Computers can be used to enable work to be done quickly and cheaply, particularly where the tasks are repetitive. This applies to work in factories and offices. In addition, an important use of computer-based systems, including robots, is in industries where the work is unpleasant, or carried out in environments unsuitable for people (see Chapter 8).

The use of computers can lead to loss of employment in some areas. However, the new technology can be used to create more wealth, and to provide more and better services for people. This will result in new opportunities for employment for people who build, maintain, program, or use the equipment.

The technology can also be used to provide employment opportunities for disabled and blind people as described below.

Aids for the disabled

Computers are having a major impact on the disabled. The compactness of the equipment makes it ideal for use at home, and many different devices can be controlled by microcomputers.

A microcomputer with disk storage, printer and word processing package, a photocopier, a telephone, and a telephone answering machine, are sufficient for a home office. A disabled person can quickly learn to use this equipment for correspondence, filing, calculation of statistics, and preparing reports. Contact can be maintained with the employer's offices through the telephone, either verbally or with the microcomputer linked via a modem to the central computer. Viewdata systems provide electronic mail facilities enabling deaf employees to communicate successfully with outside offices.

A blind programmer has helped to develop a computer which has a keyboard for input and a tactile strip for feed-back of information from the computer in braille. The equipment can also be used as a terminal to larger computers. This type of system gives a level of independence to a blind programmer equal to that of a sighted person.

Training aids are available for handicapped children enabling them to draw using a touch-sensitive keyboard for inputting commands linked to a microcomputer-controlled turtle (as described in Chapter 9). When a key is touched, the microcomputer interprets this as an instruction. Other devices output sound so that these can be recognised and copied by the children.

Implications for health care

Computers are used extensively in the health service including general practice, hospitals and community medicine. The data processing capability of computer systems is used for scheduling services, appointments and visits, and for maintaining medical records and indexes. Pharmacy systems are used for stores and ordering.

There is a need for communicating information, for example, data needs to be sent from wards to general practitioners, between departments in hospitals, from one hospital to another, and between regions. Microcomputers can be placed where they are needed locally, and linked through local area networks or digital telephone exchanges. Viewdata systems can also provide a useful means of communicating information.

The control capabilities of computers also have a variety of applications. For example, computers can be used to monitor and control blood pressure. Another application is a touch-sensitive, computer-controlled hoist for lifting patients in hospitals.

Expert systems

Computers can be programmed to act as 'experts' in fields as diverse as medical diagnosis and oil exploration.

These types of systems are also known as *intelligent knowledge-based systems* (IKBS), since the knowledge of an expert in a particular field has to be stored in the computer system, and tapped by a user having an 'intelligent conversation' with the computer.

There are many difficulties in building this type of system. The computer system has to be designed to process complex programs quickly. The programs interact with the user by displaying questions and interpreting the user's answers in an intelligent way. Eventually, by a logical process, the system provides the correct answers to the user's problem. This type of programmed intelligence is known as artificial intelligence (AI), and specialised programming languages are used in this area, for example, LISP (List Processing) and PROLOG.

The user needs to communicate with the computer in a natural way, so there is a need for the 'conversation' to be carried out using

English words and sentences, and for easy input of commands and responses through special keys, perhaps with pictures on them, or light pens for selecting options on the screen. Alternatively touch-sensitive screens may be used.

Some systems are already in use, particularly in the medical field. Experiments in medical diagnosis have shown that a patient may prefer to communicate with the computer using this type of system. However, doctors need to provide the expert information in the first place, and still need to use their experience to verify the diagnosis, and to treat the patient.

IT initiatives

The importance of Information Technology has been recognised by governments and other bodies which have initiated various programmes to promote awareness and research in this area.

In the UK, various awareness, consultancy and pilot schemes have been sponsored and organised by the Department of Trade and Industry (DTI), the Department of Education and Science (DES), the National Computer Centre (NCC), and professional bodies.

The range of subjects covered by these schemes includes:

MAP Microelectronics Applications Project, providing support for courses and consultancy to encourage the use of microelectronics in processes and products

CADCAM Computer Aided Design/Computer Aided Manufacturing, a scheme for industry that offers demonstrations at firms, grants for consultancy and research/development, as well as support for courses (see Chapter 8).

Office Automation Pilot and Demonstration Systems Various systems have been installed in the public sector to monitor user experience and assess benefits.

In addition to these projects, the application of new technologies in industry is actively being encouraged by several complementary schemes, by the DTI in particular. Support for computer work in schools is discussed in Chapter 9.

Business users can obtain help through college courses, and from

NCC Microsystems Centres which give free access to a range of computer equipment and software

Research into various aspects of IT is being sponsored by the UK government following the recommendations of the Alvey Committee (whose report *A Programme for Advanced Information Technology* was published by HMSO in 1982). Funding for research is also provided through the EEC's European Strategic Programme for Research and Development in Information Technology (ESPRIT).

The widespread use of home computers, and microcomputers in companies, is leading to experiments in Distance Learning. These schemes are designed to enable students to learn away from colleges, using microcomputers with telesoftware, video tapes or discs, suitable textbooks, and learning notes. This type of learning can be supplemented by weekend courses, tutorials, and additional practical work on computer equipment in colleges.

Glossary of Computing Terms

Accumulator   A storage location in which arithmetic results are accumulated.

Acoustic coupler   A device attached to a portable terminal or computer, into which a telephone handset is inserted to allow information to be passed acoustically over the telephone line to a remote computer system.

Ada   A high-level programming language named after Lady Ada Lovelace, the 'first computer programmer'.

A/D converter   Analog/digital converter; converts analog (continuous) signals, usually from sensors measuring temperature, voltage, etc., to digital (binary) signals for processing by a computer.

Address   The unique identification of a specific storage location in the computer's memory.

AI   Artificial Intelligence; the ability to work out implied rules from a set of examples of decisions taken by experts.

ALU   The arithmetic and logic unit of the central processor which performs calculations and compares values during the processing of data.

APL   A Programming Language; a high-level programming language.

ASCII   American Standard Code for Information Interchange by which characters (for example, letters, punctuation and numerals) are coded into binary.

Assembler   A program which converts a low-level language program into machine code.

Backing storage   All forms of storage that are external to the main store.

Back-up copy The copy of a program or data on disk or tape in case the original becomes damaged or altered accidentally.

Bar code A code represented by a succession of printed bars found particularly on supermarket items; the code is 'read' optically by passing a sensing pen connected to a computer over the lines.

BASIC Beginners All-purpose Symbolic Instruction Code; a high-level programming language.

Binary notation The representation of decimal numbers using only 0s and 1s of the mathematical system known as the binary code.

Bit A binary digit.

Byte A group of binary digits, usually eight bits.

C A high-level programming language.

CADCAM Computer Aided Design/Computer Aided Manufacturing.

CADMAT Computer Aided Design Manufacture and Test.

CAL Computer Assisted Learning.

Cartridge A plug-in module containing ROM and/or RAM.

CCITT The International Telegraph and Telephone Consultative Committee.

Ceefax A videotex system broadcast by the BBC.

Central processing unit (CPU) The unit comprised of the ALU, control unit and memory.

Centronics parallel interface An interface commonly used for connecting printers to computers.

Character A particular alphanumeric symbol such as a letter of the alphabet, punctuation mark or numeral.

Check digit A digit introduced into a standard code, that allows the computer to test for transposition of the digits in the code whenever entered by a user.

Chip An electronic circuit produced on a single piece of semiconductor based material, for example, silicon; also called a microchip, silicon chip, or integrated circuit.

Clock The circuit that produces regular electronic pulses that enables the operation of all units of a computer to be synchronised.

COBOL COmmon Business Oriented Language; a high-level programming language.

COM Computer output onto microfiche or film.

COMAL COmmon Algorithmic Language; a high-level programming language.

Compiler   A program that is loaded into main memory to convert a program written in a high-level language to machine code.

Composite video   A form of video output from a computer that combines the red, green and blue signals into one signal.

Control unit   The part of the central processing unit which accesses program instructions, interprets them, and controls their execution.

CPP   Critical Path Planning.

Cursor   A marker on the VDU screen which indicates where the next character will be displayed.

D/A converter   Converts digital to analog signals (see also A/D converter).

Daisy-wheel printer   A printer that has the character set on the circumference of a spinning wheel which moves across the paper.

Data base   A systematic, inter-related set of data files that allows combinations of data to be selected as requested by different users.

Data entry terminal   A terminal that is primarily designed to allow for input to a computer system rather than to receive output from the computer.

DBA   Data Base Administrator.

DBMS   Data Base Management System.

Digital tracer   An A/D converter that converts the movement of a tracing head into digital code for processing by the computer.

Digitising pad   A pad that senses the path of a hand-held pen from a matrix of switches beneath the writing surface.

Disk   A backing storage device that has information stored magnetically on concentric tracks over the surfaces of the disk.

Dot matrix printer   A printer which forms characters as a matrix of dots.

Dumping   The copying of data in a backing store as a security measure.

EFT   Electronic Funds Transfer.

Electronic mail   A means of transmitting messages electronically.

Electronic spreadsheet   A particular type of applications package that allows users to design their own worksheets directly on the screen.

EPROM   Erasable Programmable Read Only Memory; an erasable form of PROM.

Execution The processing by the computer of programmed instructions.

Execution error An error detected during the execution of a program.

Expert system A computer system which stores the knowledge of experts and allows easy access to this.

Expression The name given to an algebraic or logical relationship.

FAX Facsimile equipment and transmission.

Field A sub-division of a record.

File An organised set of records.

Floppy disk A single pliable disk, usually contained in a protective sleeve, used for storing programs and data.

Flowchart A diagrammatic representation of the logic of a program.

FORTH A language for writing programs requiring fast processing.

FORTRAN FORmula TRANslator; a high-level programming language.

Graph plotter An output device that selects and uses a pen, thereby allowing continuous lines and coloured charts to be produced.

Hardware The physical devices making up a computer system, as opposed to software.

Help system Procedures built into software to provide messages to the user when requested.

High-level language A term applied to a programming language in which each instruction corresponds to several machine code instructions; such a language often consists of English words and mathematical symbols.

High-Resolution graphics A graphics display based upon the individual pixels making up a screen area.

Icon A small picture displayed on a screen to indicate a computer function.

IEEE-488 A standard interface for linking printers and scientific instruments to computers.

Image processing The conversion of optically captured images to digital form.

Ink-jet printer   A printer which forms the characters by electrically charging drops of ink.

Integrated business system   A number of software packages linked together and used for processing a company's business applications.

Integrated circuit (IC)   *See* chip.

Interpreter   A program that is loaded into main memory, or available in ROM, to convert instructions written in a high-level programming language to machine code; an interpreter is different from a compiler since each instruction is executed immediately after it has been translated into machine code.

IPs   Information Providers; the providers of information in a videotex system.

IT   Information Technology.

Joystick   A hand-held stick that pivots at its base; the movement of the stick causes a corresponding movement in the same direction of a character on the VDU screen.

Light pen   A device used for selecting items or drawing on a computer's screen.

Line printer   A printer on a computer system that prints a line at a time.

LISP   List Processing; a high-level programming language used for artificial intelligence applications.

Local area network (LAN)   The interconnection of several computers and associated devices within local distances, which can communicate with each other.

Logical error   A mistake in the logic of a program causing wrong results.

LOGO   A high-level programming language which allows shapes and pictures to be drawn using simple commands.

Machine code   The binary instruction code used by the central processor in a particular machine.

Magnetic stripe   A stripe of magnetic material, sometimes added to the price label of items, encoded and scanned by a hand-held pen (also known as a wand).

Magnetic tape   A type of backing storage on which information is stored magnetically; the tape may be in cassette form or spooled for reel-to-reel use.

Main store   The central storage area coupled directly to the CPU which is used for holding the operating system and the program instructions to be executed, as well as the data currently being processed.

MAP   Microelectronics Applications Project.

Menu   A list of options displayed on a computer's screen from which the user can select the particular function required.

MICR   Magnetic Ink Character Recognition code; for example, printed along the bottom of cheques using ink that can be magnetised so that the coding can be read directly into a computer system.

Microprocessor   A central processing unit designed as a single chip used in microcomputers and in the control system of some industrial and domestic equipment.

Modem   A modulator-demodulator; a device used to convert digital signals into audio signals (modulate) before transmission over, for example, a telephone line, and to convert received audio signals into digital form (demodulate) for use by a computer system.

Mouse   A device with wheels or a track ball which can be moved over a desk-top to cause a cursor to move on the computer's screen in a related way.

MRP   Materials Requirements Planning.

MSDOS   A disk operating system from Microsoft.

Object-oriented programming   A type of programming which deals with objects and messages rather than data and processing.

OCR   Optical Character Recognition; a method used to input printed characters into a computer system by scanning them with light-sensitive heads that 'read' each character.

Office automation   Using computers and communications equipment to automate administrative procedures.

Operating system   A program used to control the functioning of a computer system.

Oracle   A videotex system broadcast by commercial television.

PABX   Private Automatic Branch Exchange; a digital switchboard.

Package   A program and associated documentation developed for an application.

Page formatting   A facility available in word-processing systems for changing margins, inserting headings and footings.

Pagination control   A facility available in word-processing systems for indicating page breaks.

Pascal   A high-level programming language named after a French mathematician, Blaise Pascal.

Password   A unique sequence of characters that needs to be entered at a terminal before a user can gain access to a computer.

PCDOS   The disk operating system available on IBM's Personal Computer.

Peripheral   The name given to any input or output device that can be connected to the main memory and CPU of any computer system.

PILOT   An authoring language used for computer assisted learning applications.

Pixel   A picture element or 'dot' on a computer's screen that can be addressed in high-resolution graphics.

POS   Point Of Sale terminal; a terminal which looks like a cash register and is used to record sales information for transmission to a computer.

Prestel   A videotex system transmitted over the public telephone system and displayed on the screen of an adapted television set by means of a direct link between the telephone and the television.

Program   A sequence of instructions that cause the computer to perform the necessary processing for a given application.

PROLOG   A high-level programming language used for artificial intelligence applications.

PROM   Programmable Read Only Memory; a programmable form of ROM.

RAM   Random Access Memory (read-addressable memory); a chip that forms part of the main memory of a computer, and that is used for holding programs and data read in from peripheral devices; the contents of RAM are lost when the power to the computer is switched off.

Record   A related set of data; the items of data are known as *fields*, and a collection of records is referred to as a *file*.

Registers   Specific storage areas in the CPU and main memory used to control the functioning of the computer, and to provide information on the present state of the processing during a computer run.

RGB   Red-Green-Blue video signal; a coloured video display is developed from three independent signals controlling the red, green and blue colour circuits.

ROM   Read Only Memory; a chip used for storing programs or data that need to be permanently incorporated into a computer; ROM retains its contents when the power to the computer is switched off.

RS232C   A serial interface commonly used for connecting printers and VDUs to computers.

Scrolling   A term used for the progressive advancement of lines of text up the screen of a VDU.

Secondary storage   *See* backing storage.

Shared-logic   A term used for word processing systems in which several VDUs are linked to a shared central processor.

Smalltalk-80   A language devised at Xerox Research for object oriented programming.

Software   A term applied to programs used by computer hardware.

Source program   A program as originally written in a high or low-level language before the computer translates it into machine code.

Spelling checker   A program used in word processing systems that checks the spelling of text against a dictionary of words held on disk.

Sprite   A high resolution area containing a customised 'design' that can be moved under program control over the surface of a VDU display without corrupting the display.

String   A sequence of characters, for example, letter, punctuation and numerals.

Structured programming   A technique used for structuring data and the associated program.

Subroutine   A group of program instructions which can be entered from several points of the program; after execution of these instructions, control returns to the program instruction following the instruction which called the subroutine.

Syntax error   An incorrect use of a programming language.

Systems analysis   The analysis of a proposed computer application that leads to the design of suitable software to be used with the associated hardware.

Telesoftware   The provision of software by means of teletex or viewdata.

Teletex   An advanced form of Telex.

Teletext   The transmission of text and diagrammatic information, broadcast by television channels, that can be received by modified television sets.

Terminal   An input-output device linked to a computer that is used for entry and processing of programs and data; some terminals may be input only or output only devices.

Time-sharing   The use of a computer system by several users, apparently simultaneously and independently.

Touch-sensitive keyboard   Used for giving commands to a computer by touching portions of the keyboard.

Touch screen   A unit which can determine the position of a finger placed against the screen.

Turtle graphics   Drawing pictures by moving the cursor ('turtle') over the screen; instructions consist of length of movement, direction and 'pen up' or 'pen down'.

UNIX   An operating system designed at Bell Laboratories.

VDU   Visual Display Unit; a device like a television screen that displays output from a computer and input if an input device, such as a keyboard, is connected.

Verify   The term applied to the checking of data in a computer system.

Videotex   The transmission of computer-based text and diagrammatic information that can be displayed on modified television sets; the transmission may be via telephone lines.

Viewdata   An alternative term for interactive videotex.

Wand   The name given to a hand-held 'pen' that is passed over bar-coded or magnetic-stripe labels; the pen 'reads' the labels and passes the information to the computer.

Winchester disk   A hard-disk unit, sealed into a case, used as an alternative to floppy disks.

Word   The number of bits that can be handled by a computer in a single step; the size of the word depends on the computer being used.

Word processor   A computer using special software for word processing.

Index